W9-AXJ-713

Bloom's
GUIDES

Gabriel García Márquez's
One Hundred Years of Solitude

The Adventures of Huckleberry Finn
All the Pretty Horses
Animal Farm
Beloved
Brave New World
The Chosen
The Crucible
Cry, the Beloved Country
Death of a Salesman
The Grapes of Wrath
Great Expectations
The Great Gatsby
Hamlet
The Handmaid's Tale
The House on Mango Street
I Know Why the Caged Bird Sings
The Iliad
Lord of the Flies
Macbeth
Maggie: A Girl of the Streets
The Member of the Wedding
Of Mice and Men
1984
One Hundred Years of Solitude
Pride and Prejudice
Ragtime
Romeo and Juliet
The Scarlet Letter
Snow Falling on Cedars
A Streetcar Named Desire
The Things They Carried
To Kill a Mockingbird

Bloom's
GUIDES

Gabriel García Márquez's
One Hundred Years of Solitude

Edited & with an Introduction
by Harold Bloom

CHELSEA HOUSE
PUBLISHERS
An imprint of Infobase Publishing

Bloom's Guides: One Hundred Years of Solitude

Chelsea House
An imprint of Infobase Publishing
132 West 31st Street
New York NY 10001

Library of Congress Cataloging-in-Publication Data
Gabriel García Márquez's One hundred years of solitude / Harold Bloom, editor.
    p. cm. — (Bloom's guides)
  Includes bibliographical references and index.
  ISBN 0-7910-8578-3 (hardcover)
  1. García Márquez, Gabriel, 1928- Cien años de soledad. I. Bloom, Harold. II. Title: Gabriel García Márquez's 100 years of solitude.
III. Series.
  PQ8180.17.A73C53233 2006
  863'.64—dc22   2006011656

Contributing Editor: Mei Chin
Cover design by Takeshi Takahashi

Printed in the United States of America
Bang EJB 10 9 8 7 6 5 4 3 2 1

Contents

Introduction

HAROLD BLOOM

Macondo, according to Carlos Fuentes, "begins to proliferate with the richness of a Colombian Yoknapatawpha." Faulkner, crossed by Kafka, is the literary origins of Gabriel García Márquez. So pervasive is the Faulknerian influence that at times one hears Joyce and Conrad, Faulkner's masters, echoed in García Márquez, yet almost always as mediated by Faulkner. *The Autumn of the Patriarch* may be too pervaded by Faulkner, but *One Hundred Years of Solitude* absorbs Faulkner, as it does all other influences, into a phantasmagoria so powerful and self-consistent that the reader never questions the authority of García Márquez. Perhaps, as Reinard Argas suggested, Faulkner is replaced by Carpentier and Kafka by Borges in *One Hundred Years of Solitude*, so that the imagination of García Márquez domesticates itself within its own language. Macondo, visionary realm, is an Indian and Hispanic act of consciousness, very remote from Oxford, Mississippi, and from the Jewish cemetery in Prague. In his subsequent work, García Márquez went back to Faulkner and Kafka; but then, *One Hundred Years of Solitude* is a miracle and could only happen once, if only because it is less a novel than it is a Scripture, the Bible of Macondo. Melquíades the Magus, who writes in Sanskrit, may be more a mask for Borges than for the author himself, and yet the gypsy storyteller also connects García Márquez to the archaic Hebrew storyteller, the Yahwist, at once the greatest of realists and the greatest of fantasists but above all the only true rival of Homer and Tolstoy as a storyteller.

My primary impression, in the act of rereading *One Hundred Years of Solitude*, is a kind of aesthetic battle fatigue, since every page is crammed full of life beyond the capacity of any single reader to absorb. Whether the impacted quality of this novel's texture is finally a virtue I am not sure, since sometimes I feel like a man invited to dinner who has been served nothing but an enormous platter of Turkish Delight. Yet it is all story, where everything conceivable and inconceivable is happening at once—from creation to apocalypse, birth to death. Roberto González Echevarría has gone so far as to surmise that in some sense it is the reader who must die at the end of the story, and perhaps it is the sheer richness of the text that serves to destroy us. Joyce half-seriously envisioned an ideal reader cursed with insomnia who would spend her life in unpacking *Finnegans Wake*. The reader need not translate *One Hundred Years of Solitude*, a novel that deserves its popularity because it has no surface difficulties whatsoever. And yet, a new dimension is added to reading by this book. Its ideal reader has to be like its most memorable personage, the sublimely outrageous Colonel Aureliano Buendía, who "had wept in his mother's womb and been born with his eyes open." There are no wasted sentences, no mere transitions, in this novel, and we must notice everything at the moment we read it. It will all cohere—at least as myth and metaphor, if not always as literary meaning.

In the presence of an extraordinary actuality, consciousness takes the place of imagination. That Emersonian maxim is Wallace Stevens' and is worthy of the visionary of *Notes Toward a Supreme Fiction* and *An Ordinary Evening in New Haven*. Macondo is a supreme fiction, and there are no ordinary evenings within its boundaries. Satire, even parody, and most fantasy—these are now scarcely possible in the United States. How can you satirize Ronald Reagan or Jerry Falwell? Pynchon's *The Crying of Lot 49* ceases to seem fantasy whenever I visit Southern California, and a ride on the New York City subway tends to reduce all literary realism to an idealizing projection. Some aspects of Latin American existence transcend even the inventions of García Márquez. (I am informed, on good authority, that the older of the Duvalier dictators of Haiti, the illustrious Papa Doc, commanded that all black dogs in his nation be destroyed when he came to believe that a principal enemy had transformed himself into a black dog.) Much that is fantastic in *One Hundred Years of Solitude* would be fantastic anywhere, but what seems unlikely to a North American critic may well be a representation of reality.

Emir Monegal emphasized that García Márquez's masterwork was unique among Latin American novels, being radically different from the diverse achievements of Julio Cortázar, Carlos Fuentes, Lezama Lima, Mario Vargas Llosa, Miguel Ángel Asturias, Manuel Puig, Guillermo Cabrera Infante, and so many more. The affinities to Borges and to Carpentier were noted by Monegal as by Arenas, but Monegal's dialectical point seems to be that García Márquez was representative only by joining all his colleagues in not being representative. Yet it is now true that, for most North American readers, *One Hundred Years of Solitude* comes first to mind when they think of the Hispanic novel in America. Alejo Carpentier's *Explosion in a Cathedral* may be an even stronger book, but only Borges has dominated the North American literary imagination as García Márquez has with his grand fantasy. We inevitably identify *One Hundred Years of Solitude* with an entire culture, almost as though it were a new *Don Quixote*, which it most definitely is not. Comparisons to Balzac and even to Faulkner are also not very fair to García Márquez; the titanic inventiveness of Balzac dwarfs the later visionary, and nothing even in Macondo is as much a negative Sublime as the fearsome quest of the Bundrens in *As I Lay Dying*. *One Hundred Years of Solitude* is more of the stature of Nabokov's *Pale Fire* and Pynchon's *Gravity's Rainbow*—latecomers' fantasies, strong inheritors of waning traditions.

Whatever its limitations, García Márquez's major narrative now enjoys canonical status as well as a representative function. Its cultural status continues to be enhanced, and it would be foolish to quarrel with so large a phenomenon. I wish to address myself only to the question of how seriously, as readers, we need to receive the book's scriptural aspect. The novel's third sentence is: "The world was so recent that things lacked names, and in order to indicate them it was necessary to point," and the third sentence from the end is long and beautiful:

> Macondo was already a fearful whirlwind of dust and
> rubble being spun about by the wrath of the biblical
> hurricane when Aureliano skipped eleven pages so as not

to lose time with facts he knew only too well, and he began to decipher the instant that he was living, deciphering it as he lived it, prophesying himself in the act of deciphering the last page of the parchment, as if he were looking into a speaking mirror.

The time span between this Genesis and this Apocalypse is seven generations, so that José Arcadio Buendía, the line's founder, is the grandfather of the last Aureliano's grandfather. The grandfather of Dante's grandfather, the crusader Cacciaguida, tells his descendant Dante that the poet perceives the truth because he gazes into that mirror in which the great and small of this life, before they think, behold their thought. Aureliano, at the end, reads the Sanskrit parchment of the gypsy, Borges-like Magus, and looks into a speaking mirror, beholding his thought before he thinks it. But does he, like Dante, behold the truth? Was Florence, like Macondo, a city of mirrors (or mirages) in contrast to the realities of the Inferno, the Purgatorio, the Paradiso? Is *One Hundred Years of Solitude* only a speaking mirror? Or does it contain, somehow within it, an Inferno, a Purgatorio, a Paradiso?

Only the experience and disciplined reflections of a great many more strong readers will serve to answer those questions with any conclusiveness. The final eminence of *One Hundred Years of Solitude* for now remains undecided. What is clear to the book's contemporaries is that García Márquez has given contemporary culture, in North America and Europe as much as in Latin America, one of its double handful of necessary narratives, without which we will understand neither one another nor our own selves.

Biographical Sketch

In the winter of 1928–29, hundreds of workers went on strike on a banana plantation in Ciénaga, Colombia. They gathered; they were fired on; hundreds were killed, and afterward the details were suppressed. The plantation was named for the Bantu word for *banana*—Macondo.

The name would become a significant one for Gabriel García Márquez, born in nearby Aracataca just before the strike. *One Hundred Years of Solitude*, his tale of Macondo—or a town of the same name, with some of the same problems—would win him the Nobel Prize for Literature in 1982.

García Márquez was born in March of 1928, the first of sixteen siblings. His father, Gabriel Eligio García, was a Conservative telegraph operator of humble origins; in the autobiography *Living to Tell the Tale*, García Márquez describes him as a young man, dressed in a tight-fitting suit and a narrow tie, who fell in love in church and expressed that love with a single rose. Gabriel Eligio García's future bride, Luisa Santiaga Márquez Iguarán, was the daughter of a Liberal colonel, with a convent education and a talent for the clavichord. Luisa's parents opposed a marriage, for García not only was a recent arrival to the town, drawn by the banana trade, but had sired several children out of wedlock. After a deluge of romantic gestures, though, they gave in, and Gabriel and Luisa became engaged. Their courtship became the basis for their son's novel *Love in the Time of Cholera* (1985).

Luisa Santiaga and Gabriel Eligio were married on the condition that they never reside in Luisa's hometown of Aracataca. Unfortunately, Luisa visited her parents while heavily pregnant; thus Gabriel García was born in his grandparents' home. Luisa and her husband left soon thereafter for the town of Riohacha, where Gabriel Eligio had set up a business, leaving their first son in her parents' care.

Gabriel was the first of twelve children, a number that would later increase to sixteen, due to the illegitimate offspring sired by Gabriel Eligio. Gabriel was a sickly youth. "I don't believe that boy will grow up," one well-intentioned person told his mother. He was cursed with weak lungs and a tendency to be frightened easily. He would not know his mother until he was five or six; and he would be raised by his grandparents until he was eight. García Márquez describes his grandfather, Colonel Nicolas Ricardo Márquez Mejía, as "the biggest eater I can remember, and the most outrageous fornicator." Colonel Márquez Mejía was upright, valiant, and lusty and had served under General Rafael Uribe Uribe during the famous War of a Thousand Days. His illegitimate children from his military career would descend on the Márquez household regularly. They were honest men who got drunk and shattered the family crockery, and were each marked by a cross of ashes upon their forehead. His grandmother Tranquilina Iguarán Cotes was a woman who inhabited a magical world, who believed in premonition, and with whom young García Márquez shared a "secret code." The Márquez mansion in Aracataca was inhabited by life-size sculptures of saints and ghosts of aunts, and every one of its rooms, according to his grandmother, was inhabited by someone who had died.

At the age of eight Gabriel García moved in with his father and mother, following the death of Colonel Márquez Mejía. His mother was a fashionable, temperamental woman, practical in contrast to his fantasy-prone grandmother. His feelings toward her fell short of love: "I knew it was my duty to love her but I felt that I did not." His father owned a succession of failing pharmacies and also had a wandering eye, which provoked jealous outbursts from his wife. Eventually, however, Luisa Santiaga would follow her mother's example and welcome her husband's illegitimate offspring as her own. Finances were tight, and as each pharmacy failed, the family would relocate to a different city.

Gabriel García Márquez went off to school, eventually finishing his baccalaureate in a school set several miles outside the mountain city of Bogotá. His first story was published several months later, on September 15, 1947, in *El Espectador*. García Márquez returned to Bogotá in 1947 to enroll in the law program at the university there. While he was there, the period in Colombian history known as La Violencia (The Violence) broke out—fifteen years of mayhem that would claim the lives of at least 200,000 people. Riots and slaughter forced the University of Bogotá to close in 1948. García Márquez then enrolled in the law program at Cartagena, but dropped out to pursue what would become a lifelong career as a journalist. He began at the Cartagena newspaper *El Universal,* then relocated to Barranquilla, where he had, on one of his trips for *El Universal,* met "three boys and an old man" who would become the most influential friends of his youth: Alvaro Semundo, Germán Vargas, Alfonso Fuenmayor, and a wise mentor from Catalonia called Ramón Vinyes. The five men called themselves the "Barranquilla group" and held intellectual court at the Café Japy, where they discussed literature and politics.

Barranquilla seems to be the Colombian city that García Márquez found most happy—sunny and Caribbean and musical, as opposed to the grim and rainy Bogotá. His family had lived there on numerous occasions. Living there as an adult, however, had bohemian charm—scraping by on miniscule wages; frolicking in the brothels at night, and politicking, writing, debating, and devouring Faulkner, Virginia Woolf, and Kafka during the day. By the age of twenty-two, as he proudly recounts in *Living to Tell the Tale,* he had survived two bouts of gonorrhea and, despite weak lungs and repeated struggles with pneumonia, was smoking sixty cigarettes a day. While he was still in Barranquilla, García Márquez's beloved grandmother died, and he returned to Aracataca with his mother to sell the once-grand Márquez estate. That journey to his childhood home, he would later say, was the seed from which so much of his fiction—most prominently *One Hundred Years of Solitude*—would germinate.

By 1952, he had published several stories and achieved a certain amount of fame with his series of articles on a sailor by the name of Velasco, the sole survivor of a shipwreck who had lived for days drinking sea water and eating cardboard playing cards. Inspired by the journey he'd made to Aracataca, García Márquez was also contemplating a novel about his family, tentatively entitled *La Casa*. He would eventually abandon this work for his 1955 novel *The Leaf Storm*, which introduced a reading public to an imaginary banana town by the name of Macondo. In 1954, he moved back to Bogotá to work as a reporter, and the next year he traveled to Rome to cover the death of a pope—who, unfortunately for the writer, recovered. He lived in several places in Europe, including Paris, London, and Russia and Eastern Europe, and befriended volatile figures such as Fidel Castro. In 1958 he chased a job prospect to Caracas, Venezuela, but he returned briefly to Colombia to marry Mercedes, whom he later referred to as his "secret girlfriend." He had asked Mercedes, the daughter of an Egyptian pharmacist, to marry him fourteen years before at a dance. He had been eighteen; she had barely reached adolescence.

The job that García Márquez had been promised in Caracas fell through, so he supported himself and his new bride by peddling encyclopedias and medical textbooks. The short story "No One Writes to the Colonel" (1958) dates to this period. His first son, Rodrigo, was born in 1959 and baptized by the famous political priest Camillo Torres, an old friend of García Márquez from his law school days in Bogotá. (Rodrigo would later be killed by guerrillas, and Torres was murdered in 1966.) In 1961 the family moved to New York, where a second son, Gonzalo, was born in the following year. *In Evil Hour* also appeared in 1962; like "No One Writes," it was based on drafts he had begun while sojourning in Paris.

In 1961, with his wife and family, he embarked on a journey through the southern United States via bus in tribute to his favorite writer, William Faulkner, and found much inspiration on the dusty Mississippi roads, which he felt had a lot of resonance with his own home. Although they next settled in Mexico, García Márquez and Mercedes spent much of the following few years rattling about on buses. En route from Mexico City to Acapulco in 1965, he seized on the idea that would become *One Hundred Years of Solitude*, the book that would be the culmination of his literary re-inventions of his Aracataca childhood. He spent the next eighteen months closeted in his studio while Mercedes sold off appliances so that their family could live. *One Hundred Years* was published in 1967 and catapulted García Márquez to instant fame.

García Márquez would have a troubled relationship with his stardom. As a journalist, he had always been generous with the media; with his newfound popularity, however, he found his privacy dogged by reporters. A collection of his early journalism was tellingly titled "When I Was Happy and Unknown." Also, with the novel's success, he realized that he was no longer writing for a limited audience of friends. "[N]ow I no longer know whom of the millions of readers I am writing for," he told a reporter. "This upsets and inhibits me." Also, though he has frequently expressed a desire to return to Colombia, his celebrity in that country made establishing any semblance of a normal existence there impossible.

At the beginning of the 1970s, García Márquez relocated to Barcelona, where he wrote *Autumn of the Patriarch* (1975). *Chronicle of a Death Foretold* was published in 1982, followed by *Love in the Time of Cholera* (1985), a tribute to his parents' courtship and the first book he composed on a computer. García Márquez relocates frequently, but probably calls Mexico City his home. He stills visits Colombia from time to time, but has yet to establish a permanent residence there. He has never given up journalism—*Clandestine in Chile* was an expose of the Chilean dictatorship, and *News of a Kidnapping* followed the kidnapping of ten Colombian diplomats by a drug trafficker. He has been politically active, and his Communist affiliations have made entry into the United States difficult. In 1982, he was awarded the Nobel Prize, which he accepted dressed as a Caribbean partygoer. At the awards ceremony he spoke about poetry and world peace; he was feted with a supply of rum courtesy of his friend Fidel Castro.

García Márquez counts among his influences Franz Kafka and Virginia Woolf, whose work was introduced to him by that "wise Catalonian" Ramón Vinyes. Critics have faulted his early work for being too studiously Kafka-esque, but *The Metamorphosis* taught him an essential lesson: the most outrageous things can be told in a completely straight fashion.

Or, in his words, "That's the way my grandma used to tell stories—the wildest things with a completely natural tone of voice." His hero, however, is William Faulkner, and a lot of *Absalom! Absalom!*—which details the rise and fall of a titled family in the American South whose descendants will eventually be consumed by fire after a century—can be seen in *One Hundred Years*. Perhaps his greatest influence is his own profession. As he once famously told *The Paris Review* in 1981:

> There's a journalistic trick which you can also apply to literature. For example, if you say there are elephants flying in the sky, people are not going to believe you. But if you say that there are 425 elephants in the sky, people will probably believe you.

The most outrageous things can be presented as the truth, but in order to make them sound believable, an author must be specific. His grandmother used to complain that an engineer who visited the house was surrounded by butterflies. When García Márquez adapted this for the character of Mauricio Babilonia in *One Hundred Years*, he colored those butterflies yellow. In many ways he has realized the dream that began when he first read *The Metamorphosis*, but in a fashion that is most un–Kafka-like. Kafka strips his outrageousness to its bare bones, whereas García Márquez elaborates. His grandmother taught García Márquez the basics for inventing a tale, but being a journalist taught him how to tell a tale well.

The Story Behind the Story

The story of how Gabriel García Márquez began writing *One Hundred Years of Solitude* is a famous one. He dreamed the first few pages of the novel on a bus to Mexico City, so vividly that he "could have dictated the first chapter word by word to a typist." (García Márquez, *One Hundred Years*, Afterword). As soon as the bus stopped, he shut himself up in his study for eighteen months, while his wife, Mercedes—who had their two young sons to care for—sold the car and pawned nearly every household appliance to pay for the endless reams of paper and cigarettes he consumed. The tale goes that when he emerged with the finished manuscript, she greeted him with ten thousand dollars' worth of bills. The couple barely had enough money to post the manuscript to its publisher in Argentina.

One Hundred Years of Solitude is even more apocryphal if one considers that García Márquez spent most of his writing life trying to create it. Since he took that journey to his childhood home, Aracataca, with his mother at the age of twenty-two, this was the story that he had been trying to write. The first thing he did when he returned from Aracataca was to puzzle out the beginnings of a personal family saga called *La Casa*. Macondo was what he called his fictive hometown; the Bantu word for "banana," it had been the name of the neighboring plantation. He claims in his autobiography that it was a name that had held him in sway since he was a child. *La Casa* would eventually be abandoned, but not Macondo, which was eventually introduced to the public in the novel *The Leaf Storm*. García Márquez would continue to revisit and reinvent Macondo in short stories such as "Big Mama's Funeral," but it is not until *One Hundred Years of Solitude* that his nostalgic reimagining of his childhood community would find its most perfect expression.

It is not astounding that García Márquez had his "Eureka experience" on a bus, because much of the years leading up to it had been spent on buses. Interestingly, a novel that never leaves the environs of its tiny village first found its inspiration on the road. In fact, García Márquez traces his first creative stirrings to trips around the dusty back roads of Mississippi, where he realized that the country of his hero William Faulkner was really not that different from his own. Much of the story's structure reflects Faulkner's *Absalom! Absalom!*, the story of a Southern mansion doomed to be swept away by winds after a century has passed. In order to relate his own past, therefore, García Márquez had probed Faulkner's.

Other literary masterpieces that he calls upon to help recount his story are *Oedipus Rex*, the Bible, *The Odyssey*, and *Don Quixote*. García Márquez has never been shy about crediting writers who have influenced him, among whom he includes Franz Kafka and Virginia Woolf. Although his early work was criticized for being too calculatingly derivative (more than one critic derided him as being 'Kafka-esque'), the literary references in *One Hundred Years* are spontaneous and organic. Just as García Márquez needed time to mull over the personalities that had been resident inside him since he was twenty-two, so he needed the time to digest those whose works he had read and admired.

There are also nods to contemporary Latin authors, for García Márquez is a responsible artist who believes in acknowledging his peers. Gabriel rents a Paris studio where Rocamadour, a character from Julio Cortázar's *Hopscotch*, "was to die," and a Carlos Fuentes character by the name of Artemio Cruz is brought up in conversation. (McNerney, 45) Numerous references are made to Alejo Carpentier, and the book's labyrinthine structure must owe more than a passing debt to Jorge Luis Borges. Most tantalizingly, García Márquez borrows from himself as often as he borrows from others. Big Mama's funeral passes through, and most famously, the young prostitute who seduces Aureliano Buendía with her obese grandmother as a pimp will get her own complex history in "Innocent Erendira."

We also cannot ignore the novel's political ramifications, for García Márquez's life—and the lives of his family—has never been far removed from national turmoil. Much of Colombia's modern history is touched on here—the War of a Thousand Days, the Treaty of Neerlandia, even Sir Francis Drake, whose landing distresses one of Úrsula's ancestors so much she sits on a hot coal stove. The character of Aureliano Buendía, it has been claimed, is modeled after the famous General Rafael Uribe Uribe, who campaigned for the Liberals during the War of a Thousand Days, and under whom García Márquez's own grandfather served.

García Márquez is openly hostile toward his country's politics. Since 1810, Colombia has been a democracy where the Liberal and Conservative parties have vied for power, leading to spates of concentrated violence. Although, as Michael Wood points out in his book, the two parties stand for firm albeit different principles (reform versus reaction, separation of church and state versus unity of church and state), both sides sacrifice their principles in the fighting. Ultimately, as Wood states, they represent "a rather narrow band of class interests, and they generated intense local loyalties and hatreds which were fiercely maintained even *against* people's own interests." (Wood, 8) This can be seen in the arbitrary changing of hands that occurs in the middle of the narrative of *One Hundred Years*. Úrsula represents the people, and although she is the procreator of the major Liberal Macondo leaders, she realizes that her own grandson, Arcadio Buendía, is a Liberal tyrant and that the only sane period is when Macondo is taken over by General Moncada, who, as a Conservative, is an ideological enemy, but as a leader is a good-tempered, reasonable man. This period of decency ends—much to Úrsula's fury—by the return of her own son Aureliano Buendía, who orders the execution of Moncada, who, in times of peace, he considers to be a friend. War, in García Márquez's opinion, makes irrational, ideological fools of the most clear-eyed of men, specifically Aureliano Buendía. But García Márquez takes his political stance one step further. His Liberals and Conservatives are hilarious in their sameness; the politics are equal parts farce and brutality, perhaps encapsulated when politics comes to Macondo for the first time. Don Apolinar Moscote, the village's first magistrate, has a falling out with José Arcadio Buendía over the silly question of whether to paint the houses blue, the color of the Conservative party, and the squabble eventually escalates into the first show of military force.

García Márquez comes down hard on these issues because political struggles, and the violence they engender, have affected him since infancy. Around the time his parents settled in Aracataca, the United Fruit Company, an American company, had begun machinations with the local banana industry, much in the same way as Mr. Herbert and Mr. Brown do in the novel, opening up the previously isolated Aracataca to outside influences and exposing it to corruption. Just like Brown and Herbert, the American heads of United Fruit lived in houses surrounded by electrified chicken wire. All this would come to a bloody climax in the winter of 1928–29, almost a year after García Márquez's birth, leaving hundreds dead and no trace of the American perpetrators. In *Living to Tell the Tale*, García Márquez recalls that their family doctor went insane as a result, because—like José Arcadio Segundo in *One Hundred Years*—he was convinced that he was the only person in town who remembered. But the banana worker massacre in *One Hundred Years of Solitude* is also a representative of La Violencia, the period in Colombian history that culminated in the deaths of over 200,000 people and that also forced a young García Márquez to flee his studies when he was in university and continued to define most of his young adult life.

It is an ambitious project—writing a novel as a political fable, in which one village is a microcosm for a nation's history. It is not always successful; the political reveries sometimes feel belabored. However, where the novel succeeds is in its mythic aspirations and, most importantly, in its intimacy. This returns focus to *One Hundred Years of Solitude* as a story of friends and family—a tale that had been brewing in its creator's heart for almost two decades. So while *One Hundred Years of Solitude* may falter sometimes in its depiction of the history of Colombia, it triumphs as a history of the author. In his autobiography, García Márquez tells us of his sister Margot who eats dirt like Rebeca, his ex-colonel grandfather who hammers gold fishes, his grandmother who makes candy animals. The grandparents were forced to relocate in Aracataca because the grandfather had killed a man in his youth. García Márquez remembers his grandfather's illegitimate sons who are marked with crosses of ashes on their foreheads and gather at the house at regular intervals to run amok, drink, and smash dishes, and his Aunt Fernanda, "virgin and martyr" (García Márquez, *Living*, 122), who sewed her own shroud and died the night it was completed.

Macondo also represents García Márquez's later itinerant life, even though *Hundred Years* never leaves its confines. For although the reader never leaves Macondo, the characters do. People travel and return with international savvy—much as García Márquez did when he went to Venezuela, London, Russia, Mexico, Rome, Paris, and New York. Chilly Fernanda hails from the highlands, a walking representation of his student days in the highland city of Bogotá. José Arcadio travels the world some fifty times over. Melquíades dies (for the first time) in a desert outside of Singapore. The banana plantation is run by Americans. Ultimately, he imports the youthful version of himself and his Barranquilla friends; he cannot go to Barranquilla, so he brings Barranquilla to Macondo, along with a raffish clique composed of Alvaro (Samundo) Germán (Vargas), Alfonso (Fuenmayor), Gabriel (with his "secret girlfriend" and his escapades to France), and Ramón Vinyes, who is referred to as the "wise Catalan."

The most fundamental figure, however, is that of García Márquez's grandmother, Mina Iguarán, who shares with Úrsula—among other things—the same maiden name. García Márquez adored his grandmother, in contrast to his own mother, about whom he writes "I knew it was my duty to love her but I felt that I did not," and who, with her jealous rages, good upbringing, and fashion sense, can be thought of as part Fernanda and part Amaranta Úrsula—both of them non-mothers, Fernanda because she is so brutal, Amaranta Úrsula because she dies before she has the chance. The most poignant episode in his autobiography comes after García Márquez's grandmother has cataract surgery, a fact that is mirrored in Úrsula's blindness:

> She opened the shining eyes of her renewed youth and summarized her joy in three words, "I can see" and she swept the room with her new eyes and enumerated each thing with admirable precision.... Only I knew that the things my grandmother enumerated were not the ones in front of her in the hospital but the ones in her bedroom in Aracataca which she knew by heart and remembered in their correct order. She never recovered her sight. (García Márquez, *Living*, 170)

Similarly, Úrsula, by memorizing the places of things, deceives her own family until her death. Not only is she a competent blind woman, she is a phenomenal one; she can find a misplaced wedding ring, for instance, that has eluded everyone else. Úrsula shares many similarities with García Márquez's grandmother: the way she makes candy animals, governs the family finances, and keeps the ever-burgeoning clan together. Like Úrsula, she is petite and feisty and derives the same pleasure from opening her doors to her husband's sons and letting them frolic and drink and smash dishes. Both women die half-insane and blind (García Márquez's grandmother died surrounded by red ants and the almond trees that her husband planted), and with their passings, the fates of both the Márquez and Buendía mansions are sealed.

Conversely, in many ways, these two women are diametrically opposed. García Márquez's grandmother embodies the qualities that the reader may long for in Úrsula: mischief, imagination, and tenderness. García Márquez's grandmother allows herself to be governed by magical codes, whereas Úrsula is a pragmatist. Úrsula clings to reality, whereas García Márquez's grandmother searches for fantasy. García Márquez's grandmother believes that girls are carried off with the laundry sheets, ghosts wander, and mechanics are surrounded by butterflies. For Úrsula such occurrences are commonplace. Mina imagines her world, but Úrsula inhabits it.

Whereas Úrsula will stop up her ears with wax to keep her tenuous hold on reality, Mina is open to magical suggestion.

But Mina is not only central to the tale; she helps tell it. Critics have called early García Márquez too studied. What plagued García Márquez for decades was not the tale itself, but how to relate it. As García Márquez himself explains, "in previous attempts to write I tried to tell the story without believing in it." His realization was that he had to write the stories "with the same expression with which my grandmother told them—with a brick face." So García Márquez's memories not only are part of the story that is *One Hundred Years*, but they are woven into the very voice with which the story is told. *One Hundred Years* is one of those rare works in which the author inhabits every fiber. In this case, however, our author does not view himself as an individual, but rather as an organic composite of the infinite places and people he has loved. With this in mind, therefore, we should consider Macondo not only as a recreation of a childhood hometown, but as the teeming community that is the author himself. Open the door to the Buendía mansion, and you will find his childhood; walk across the street to the bookstore and the brothel, and you will find his reckless youth; circumnavigate the village and you will find the hurly-burly country that spawned him; walk into the Buendía mansion, and there you will find the grandmother who taught him how to tell stories. Indeed, it is her intonations that we hear ringing in our ears now.

List of Characters

The *dramatis personae* of *One Hundred Years of Solitude* is so complex that most editions begin with a Buendía family tree. The most significant characters, listed below, can be grouped into seven generations.

The founders of the Buendía clan are the first generation:

José Arcadio Buendía is the founder of Macondo and the Buendía patriarch. Driven out of his home village after killing a man, he burns for exploration and scientific innovation; after leading an intrepid team of settlers to found Macondo, he shows remarkable skill in civil planning. He forms a decades-long bond with the itinerant Melquíades, who introduces him to exotic instruments of science, and he pursues one well-meant but implausible scheme after another. Eventually, he seems to go mad, speaking incomprehensibly in Latin, and the family ties him to the chestnut tree in front of the house. He lives out his days under that tree forgotten, in solitude but for the company of ghosts.

Úrsula Iguarán, wife of José Arcadio Buendía, is arguably the central character of the book. She is also José Arcadio's cousin, in a family in which incestuous unions are cursed with pig-tailed children. Ultimately, it is because she refuses to bed him that José Arcadio must kill a man to preserve his honor, and his exile begins.

Although José Arcadio Buendía is the explorer, it is Úrsula, searching for a runaway son, who discovers the first route *out* of Macondo. While her husband squanders their money on exotic scientific instruments, she keeps the family solvent by selling candy animals and pastries. As the house decomposes, Úrsula fights back. When war claims virtually all the adult males, Úrsula raises legions of children—legitimate, illegitimate, and adopted—and she keeps the Buendías out of trouble through the numerous Liberal and Conservative administrations. She despises politics, tends the fires of memory, and is vigilant against incest, and her behavior implies a religious traditionalism bordering on superstition. Sprightly, practical, and small in size, she lives well past one hundred years—outliving all her progeny and most of theirs. In later years she hides her blindness by memorizing every detail of the house, and it is not long after her death that the Buendía clan begins to crumble.

Two more early inhabitants of Macondo will play key roles throughout the book:

Pilar Ternera is the village soothsayer and the village whore, although she does not charge for her services. A woman with a hoarse, crow-like laugh and a persistent smell of smoke, she is one of Macondo's founding members. She claims the virginity of the first generation of Buendía boys and is the mother of illegitimate sons Arcadio (by José Arcadio) and Aureliano José (by Aureliano). In addition, she acts as matchmaker for some of the story's key unions—Aureliano Buendía and Remedios, and the last Aureliano and Amaranta Úrsula. Important figures like Úrsula rely on her Tarot readings to make decisions. In many ways she is Úrsula's less virtuous double—Pilar is the whore while Úrsula is the wife, but both are mothers and authority figures. Pilar actually outlives Úrsula. In the words of García Márquez, when she dies, the village dies with her.

Melquíades is the leader of a troupe of gypsies that comes to Macondo just after the town's birth. He is the most powerful figure in the book, a man who has traveled the world and can perform wonders, changing shape or even returning from the dead. Prophet, creator, mischief maker, he predicts Macondo's history in mysterious manuscripts not meant to be understood until the town's final hours. Though he dies—twice—he never leaves the story, as his ghost is a frequent visitor to the Buendía household and his memory, like his parchments, remains in his study.

José Arcadio Buendía and Úrsula Iguarán have three children of their own (José Arcadio, Aureliano, and Amaranta) and adopt one (Rebeca), so the second generation contains four, plus Aureliano's wife:

José Arcadio is the first child and the elder. He is born en route to Macondo, *without* a pig's tail—much to Úrsula's relief. He develops into a physically powerful and magnificently endowed man; after a gypsy girl lures him out of Macondo, he disappears for years, traveling the world. He returns covered with tattoos and earns a living by prostituting himself to local women. Rebeca, his adopted sister, falls for his brute charm, and although Úrsula banishes them from the household, their marriage is a happy one. José Arcadio later begins to appropriate arable land around the couple's house—land already owned by others in the town—and he dies mysteriously, shot in the head. (Note that José Arcadio's father, the original José Arcadio Buendía, is always referred to by the full name—the younger José Arcadio, never.)

(Colonel) Aureliano Buendía, the second son of José Arcadio Buendía and Úrsula, is a silent, introverted man with a talent for precognition—the first of the novel's Aurelianos, all of whom, as Úrsula observes, are born and die with their eyes open. He works as a goldsmith until the tragic death of his child-wife, Remedios, turns him to a career of military campaigning and politics. He sires one son, Aureliano José, by Pilar Ternera, and, after becoming a subversive national hero, seventeen more by women throughout the region. Ultimately he finds futility in war and returns to his gold work.

Remedios Moscote becomes Aureliano's wife. She is the youngest daughter of Don Apolinar Moscote, Macondo's first official magistrate and thus José Arcadio Buendía's rival. At nine years of age, Remedios captivates Aureliano, and it is for her that he crafts the first of his endless gold fishes. Remedios is afraid of Aureliano more than attracted to him, and the marriage is postponed until menses, which at last she greets with childlike glee; but their union does not last long, as Remedios dies in childbirth. Her bedroom in the Buendía household is haunted by her moldering dolls for years afterward, and until the end of the book a lamp is kept burning beneath a daguerreotype of a young Remedios in ribbons.

Amaranta, the one legitimate daughter in the second Buendía generation, begins life as a normal girl, talented at embroidery. Her life is defined by frustrated love for Pietro Crespi, the dance instructor she shares with adopted sister Rebeca; after Crespi chooses Rebeca, Amaranta schemes first against their marriage and then against Rebeca's life. She later spurns Crespi, causing his suicide; she burns her hand in remorse and bears the black bandage ever after. Despite a protracted courtship with Aureliano's friend Gerineldo Márquez and dalliances with two nephews, Amaranta spends her life in solitude, hardened by resentment. In later years she helps to raise and educate the household's children, and she foresees her own death in sufficient time to prepare quietly.

Rebeca comes to the Buendía household mute and strange, bearing a rocking chair, a bag containing her parents' bones, and a habit of eating dirt. Úrsula adopts her as her own daughter. When Rebeca grows up, her affair with the Italian Pietro Crespi sparks Amaranta's eternal jealousy. But Rebeca's fierce sexual urges find satisfaction not with her priggish fiancé, but with her gigantic, tattooed, macho adopted older brother José Arcadio. After José Arcadio's mysterious death, Rebeca locks herself in their house and spends her the rest of her life in decay.

José Arcadio has no children by Rebeca, but he does have a son by Pilar Ternera, part of the third generation:

(José) Arcadio, the son of José Arcadio by Pilar Ternera, is the first child of the second generation of Buendías. He is a lonely boy, ridiculed for his womanish buttocks, and he keeps to himself at home. He is the first Buendía to converse with the ghost of Melquíades. When Colonel Aureliano Buendía departs for war and leaves Arcadio in charge, Arcadio becomes a tyrant—strutting around in braided epaulettes, flogging the Moscote family, ordering random executions and imprisonments, and putting the local priest under house arrest. Not knowing that she is his mother, he chases Pilar Ternera. In desperation, Ternera introduces him to one of the local virgins—Santa Sofía de la Piedad, by whom he fathers two sons and a daughter. When the Conservatives retake Macondo, Arcadio is court-martialed and shot.

Santa Sofía de la Piedad sells her virginity to Arcadio for fifty pesos, and by him she ultimately becomes mother to three Buendías: Remedios the Beauty and twins José Arcadio Segundo and Aureliano Segundo. After Arcadio's execution she moves into the Buendía household, where she becomes one of the clan's most enduring members—though, thanks to her "rare virtue of never existing completely except at the opportune moment," everyone tends to forget she is there. Ever in the shadows, she cooks, cleans, and even nurses Úrsula on her deathbed; but in the end, even her own daughter-in-law does not remember their relationship. In the house's later stages of decay, realizing the cause is lost, Santa Sofía de la Piedad simply walks out, and she is not missed.

Colonel Aureliano Buendía has no children by Remedios, but he has eighteen in total, also part of the third generation:

Aureliano José, his son by Pilar Ternera, is raised by the Colonel's sister Amaranta, for whom he eventually fosters an incestuous passion—unfortunate because Buendía legend dictates that incestuous unions yield pig-tailed progeny. Frustrated, Aureliano José departs for war, only to be rejected for good by his aunt when he returns. He dies through a mistake in the cards—taking a bullet destined for another man.

The 17 Aurelianos are the miscellaneous sons of Colonel Aureliano Buendía, born to seventeen different women during his military campaigns. There are mulatto Aurelianos;

effeminate Aurelianos; enterprising Aurelianos who bring a railroad and an ice factory to Macondo. Each Aureliano as a child is taken to the Buendía mansion to be baptized, and from time to time they all congregate at the mansion to drink and party. One Ash Wednesday the local priest marks their foreheads with crosses of ash; these cannot be scrubbed off and ultimately are their undoing. After the Colonel insults the banana company, every one of the seventeen is assassinated by the banana company's thugs.

The fourth generation comprises the three children of Arcadio and Santa Sofía de la Piedad: Remedios the Beauty and twins José Arcadio Segundo and Aureliano Segundo:

Remedios the Beauty is the most fatally beautiful woman in Macondo, if not the entire world. Because of her, men shoot themselves, fall to their deaths from the roofs, and are otherwise reduced to madness and destitution. Remedios herself is a simpleton, or a free spirit, who shaves her head, eats with her fingers, and prefers to wander around naked. In the end, she is carried off to the heavens by the wind while hanging sheets to dry.

José Arcadio Segundo and **Aureliano Segundo**—García Márquez was fascinated with scientific studies of twins, and he explores this theme through Arcadio's two sons. Born after their father's death, the Segundo twins begin life indistinguishable, mature into opposites, and die identical once again. It is hypothesized that they might have switched identities as children, because José Arcadio Segundo exhibits traits of the Aurelianos and vice versa.

Aureliano Segundo amasses a fortune through raffles and the preternatural fertility of his livestock, becomes a gourmand, and sets up house with mistress Petra Cotes. He continues his relationship with Petra after his marriage to the beautiful but demanding Fernanda del Carpio. Later in life, his relationship with Petra matures into happy domesticity, and they end up taking care of Fernanda.

José Arcadio Segundo is a recluse who finds his calling battling the corrupt heads of the banana company. In the end he is the one of two survivors of the banana company massacre. Being the only Macondo witness to a three-thousand-person slaughter that everyone else has forgotten drives him mad. He cloisters himself in Melquíades' old study, converses with the dead gypsy, and becomes the first Buendía to attempt to decipher the manuscripts that Melquíades left behind.

At the end of the twins' life, they revert to the synchronicity that characterized their boyhood. Aureliano Segundo slims down to José Arcadio Segundo's size and develops a conscience. They expire at the same moment and are buried in each other's grave.

Petra Cotes is a golden-eyed, sensuous mulatto who makes her living raffling animals and has a preternatural power to bring fertility simply by walking past the pens. She becomes involved with José Arcadio Segundo but beds Aureliano Segundo by accident, mistaking him for his twin. Eventually, she becomes Aureliano Segundo's permanent lover, even throughout his marriage. But when Aureliano Segundo develops a conscience, so does she; and when he dies, she continues to take care of his widow, Fernanda, by anonymously sending baskets of food.

Born in the highlands, **Fernanda del Carpio** was raised by religious parents to believe that she would become the queen of Madagascar. She uses a gold chamber pot with the family crest, weaves funeral wreaths as a family business, and dines off of silver and china. She comes to Macondo during a festival to usurp the crown of Remedios the Beauty, the festival queen a plan that ends in bloodshed. Aureliano Segundo tracks her back to the highlands and brings her back to Macondo as his wife. Fernanda is snobbish, neurotic, pretentious, and dogmatically religious. She makes love to her husband through a slit in her nightgown, fills the house with plaster saints, and drives Úrsula crazy with her rules. She and Petra Cotes are opposites. She is the wife, the mother, and the aristocrat; Petra Cotes is the seemingly infertile, working-class girl whose company Fernanda's husband prefers.

Of the three, only Aureliano Segundo continues the line. The fifth generation comprises his three children with Fernanda del Carpio:

Renata Remedios ("Meme") is the oldest daughter of Aureliano Segundo and Fernanda, and cherished by her father. Although her mother insists on naming her after her ancestors—Renata was Fernanda's mother's name—the family calls her "Meme," hoping to avoid the curse that seems to come with the Buendía tradition of repetitive names. Meme is the most balanced of the Buendías—a well-adjusted and popular girl who dances, plays the clavichord to please her mother, and chats with her girlfriends about boys. She falls in love with local mechanic Mauricio Babilonia and sees him, with the help of Pilar Ternera, despite her mother's interdiction. Fernanda learns that the two have been making love during Meme's bath time and arranges for Mauricio to be shot in the back; she locks Meme in a convent, where Meme does not speak another word for the rest of her life. The nuns later appear with Meme's infant son, Aureliano Babilonia, whom Fernanda conceals.

José Arcadio (II)—The only son of Aureliano Segundo and Fernanda, José Arcadio is an asthmatic invalid who grows up in terror of saints and family ghosts. Like Aureliano José before him, he develops an early infatuation with Amaranta, his great-grand-aunt. It is in him that Úrsula and Fernanda's hopes reside; they perfume him and raise him to be the next pope. He is sent to Rome, where he tries to obliterate all memory of Amaranta by living a debauched life. He returns upon hearing of the death of his mother, and immediately transforms the fallen Buendía mansion into a lusty playhouse, where he cavorts with children in a swimming pool filled with champagne. Eventually his appetites destroy him; the children drown him in his own bath.

Amaranta Úrsula is the youngest daughter, and the only girl to be named after either Amaranta or Úrsula. She seems to combine all of the best Buendía feminine traits: she is stylish and beautiful, with Amaranta's cleverness and talent for needlework and Úrsula's boundless energy. Aureliano Segundo, who dotes on her, sends her to Brussels, where she marries a man known only as Gaston. Upon her return with her husband, however, she enters into a torrid affair with her nephew, Aureliano Babilonia. Despite the undertones of incest that run throughout, this is the only incestuous affair in *One Hundred Years of Solitude* that is consummated. Amaranta Úrsula dies giving birth to a baby with the pig's tail that Úrsula always feared—and with her death begins the end of Macondo.

The sixth generation contains only Meme's illegitimate son by Mauricio Babilonia:

Aureliano Babilonia has no idea of his parentage, so when he falls in love with Amaranta Úrsula, he does not know that he is sleeping with his aunt. His last name, Babilonia, suggests Babylon, implying that Aureliano Babilonia will be the man in charge during the fall. The ghost of Melquíades supervises his education, and ultimately, as Macondo falls around him, he is the one to decipher the gypsy's manuscripts.

The affair between Amaranta Úrsula and her nephew, Aureliano Babilonia, produces one ill-fated child, the seventh and last Buendía generation:

Aureliano Amaranta Úrsula's son by her sister's son, is the last Buendía. He emerges with a pig's tail, killing his mother in the process. Left alone in Aureliano Babilonia's grief, he does not survive his first day. His corpse is carried away by the legions of ants whose invasions Amaranta Úrsula, like Úrsula before her, tried to prevent.

Summary and Analysis

"Many years later as he faced the firing squad, Colonel Aureliano Buendía was to remember the distant afternoon when his father took him to discover ice."

Sweeping opening lines are a signature of almost any ambitious author. Such sentences skip the usual introductions, and without explanation, plunge the reader straight into another world. They both set up the story and tie it together; by rule, they should not be flowery, but terse and overwhelming. If the sentence works, it puts its author into a league with Tolstoy and Dickens. In García Márquez's case, he tosses us politics, impending death, and scientific discovery before even pausing for punctuation.

With these few words, therefore, García Márquez somewhat arrogantly toots his own horn: *One Hundred Years of Solitude* will not be a *good* book, but a brilliant one. It will not be bound by the rules of chronology and character; it will start at the end and work its way how it pleases. In its theme, *One Hundred Years of Solitude* is not a story about people, but of humankind; Genesis crystallized into one small Colombian village over a period of a hundred years. It is a parable of genetics, for no matter how hard the village of Macondo tries to preserve its solitude, it needs the infiltration of the outside world to survive. It is political, a fable of Colombian civil strife. It is self-referential, where other authors' works (e.g., Fuentes and Cortobar) make winking cameos. It is mischievous and absurd, an upside-down tale about an upside-down world where dead angels, Lazarus-like resurrections, and restless ghosts are matter-of-fact, but clocks, telescopes, magnets, and ice are objects of fear and wonder. At its heart, however, and despite its ambitions, it is an intimate project, an elegy to the village of García Márquez's youth, told in the deadpan fashion that resonates with the voice of the author's own grandmother. The characters that populate the story—the devastating beauty next door carried away to heaven, the man surrounded by

33

butterflies, the enigmatic Colonel—are all people whom García Márquez experienced when he was growing up.

Everything in *One Hundred Years* is cyclical. It will take seven chapters for Colonel Aureliano Buendía to get back to the firing squad he faces in the first sentence. An unknown commander shoots himself underneath a young girl's window; an aunt watches her already-grown nephew shave in the mirror. Another character is introduced to us with his deathbed thoughts. There is no conventional suspense, because we know endings before anything begins. Macondo activities are circular; Aureliano Buendía melts his gold fishes at the end of the day so he can re-weld them in the morning. Amaranta weaves and unravels her shroud. Even the language plays with time; Úrsula is described as a "newborn" old lady; Fernanda is a "widow whose husband had still not died," and Remedios is a nine-year-old great-great-grandmother. Buendía offspring do not vanish when they die; they just repeat themselves, both in names and in traits. Multiple generations of nephews fall in love with their aunts, multiple generations of brothers share mistresses, multiple Aurelianos are born wide-eyed and silent, multiple José Arcadios are born lusty and tragic. It is García Márquez's bawdy exaggeration of the oft-heard family phrase "You are just like your father." In Macondo, sons are not *like* their fathers; in some cases, they *are* their fathers. Clairvoyance reverberates throughout the book, but it is a more reliable art than usual, for looking into the future is the same as looking into the past. Ultimately, the patriarch José Arcadio Buendía will go mad because he realizes exactly this: time in Macondo does not progress, but loops around. "It is as if the world were repeating itself," observes Úrsula.

Briefly, a note on the book's organization: Although not done explicitly by the author, the book can be divided into four sections of roughly five chapters each. Chapters 1 through 5 deal with Macondo in its first innocent heyday and also its founding as a real town, in that there is birth, marriage, disease, communication with the outside world, and death. Chapter 6, which begins again with Colonel Aureliano Buendía's future, focuses on Macondo in political turmoil. By the time chapter 9 concludes, Aureliano has fulfilled everything the first sentence of chapter 6 has promised. Chapter 10, the halfway point, echoes the opening sentence by beginning with another Aureliano, Aureliano Segundo, and his memories as he, like the Colonel before him, faces death. The rest of the section focuses on Aureliano Segundo, his twin José Arcadio Segundo, and Aureliano Segundo's offspring and replaces internal politics (the war between the Liberals and the Conservatives) with capitalism (the American banana company) as the central tension. Chapter 15, with typical aplomb, announces the end of Macondo and introduces the last adult Aureliano. Although chapters 15 through 20 detail Macondo's downfall, they also mirror the village's beginning, as if the town must be unwoven in exactly the way it was created. It is the first section in rewind. The last Aureliano is a duplicate of his namesake, just as his lover Amaranta Úrsula is a copy of the founding matriarch. The Buendía house must be restored to its former splendor before it can fall; the inhabitants must leave in much the same order with which they first came so Macondo can be reduced to the solitude in which it first began.

SECTION I: Chapters 1–5

Chapter 1 is a portrait of Macondo's founder, José Arcadio Buendía. The Genesis/origin of humankind influence is evident—Macondo's inhabitants lack the language to describe their world and are reduced to pointing. The founder of this town, José Arcadio Buendía, is a man seized with invention and hare-brained schemes; he is also a man who has fallen under the spell of the gypsies, an eerie band headed by the prophetic, mysterious Melquíades. Melquíades is Satan/snake, for he introduces José Arcadio Buendía to the knowledge that is science and intellect and also to the restlessness that such knowledge inevitably brings. ("It's the smell of the devil," Úrsula declares when she surprises Melquíades in his laboratory.) First Melquíades introduces José Arcadio Buendía to magnets. The overly excitable patriarch purchases them because he believes that they can call gold from the ground.

Quickly José Arcadio Buendía passes into the Age of Enlightenment. He buys a magnifying glass because he thinks it can be sold as a war weapon. He declares that the world is round. He experiments with alchemy, and, with the help of Melquíades, he builds a laboratory for the distilling of elements and other such disastrous experiments.

José Arcadio Buendía also proves himself to be quite the civil engineer, for Macondo is a beautifully functioning town, where everyone is fed and happy and no one dies. Nonetheless, Macondo is still a temporary settlement, for José Arcadio Buendía has succumbed to the itch for exploration; he is still questing for his paradise, and in his mind, Macondo is just a stop along the way. His expeditions are frustrated when he comes across the ruins of a Spanish galleon, seemingly moored in the jungle—a sign that the sea is not far away and that Macondo is surrounded by the ocean in all sides. (This would not explain how the residents got there to begin with, nor how the gypsies are able to make their regular pilgrimages.) These journeys do not come without immense financial strains. Úrsula, his formidable wife, finally puts an end to them by claiming that she will die if they do not settle in Macondo permanently. Not long after, the gypsies return with the news that their leader, Melquíades, is dead from fever in the Singapore desert. It would appear that Macondo has reached its first period of peace. Its founder resigns himself to staying and no longer has his old friend to egg him on. But the peace is only temporary. Melquíades may be dead, but his followers still come bearing strange inventions, enabling José Arcadio Buendía—now forbidden to explore abroad—to explore at home. Among the wondrous things the gypsies bring is ice, which brings us back full circle to the chapter's opening and to Aureliano Buendía's childhood memory. Not surprisingly, mirrors, and objects with mirror-like properties—including ice—all reappear throughout repetitive Macondo. Ice, however, is particularly appropriate. Like Macondo, ice is an illusion—it sparkles like a diamond and burns to the touch, but when it disappears it is without a trace.

Chapter 2 skips back to before Macondo's founding and to the Buendía marriage that starts it all. Úrsula and José Arcadio Buendía are native to the village of Riohacha. Their union is not a new one—their lines have mixed for time eternal, incest being a recurrent motif in the story. Úrsula and José Arcadio Buendía are in fact cousins. The tradition of such incestuous unions is ill-fated, however. Úrsula's aunt married José Arcadio Buendía's uncle, and their offspring was born with a pig's tail, a boy who met an early death when his butcher chum attempted to remove it with a whack of the knife. Úrsula marries José Arcadio Buendía but, terrified by her mother's warnings, refuses to have intercourse, fending off his attempts with a chastity belt made of sail cloth, leather straps, and an iron buckle. Meanwhile, perhaps in order to assuage his sexual frustration, José Arcadio Buendía pursues his hobby of raising fighting cocks. When one of his cocks beats the cock of a man named Prudencio Aguilar, the enraged Prudencio Aguilar insults his opponent, insinuating what all the town knows—that Úrsula, after one year of marriage, is a virgin—and suggesting that maybe José Arcadio Buendía's is frustrated not by a chastity belt, but by his own inadequacy. José Arcadio Buendía kills Aguilar with a spear, and spear in hand, persuades his wife to remove her chastity garment, and the couple consummate their marriage for the first time.

Unfortunately, the ghost of Aguilar haunts José Arcadio Buendía and effectively drives him out of his Eden, in this case his family home of Riohacha, together with a handful of restless inhabitants and their families. The route that they travel is not clear, because after they get to Macondo, José Arcadio Buendía is never, in his lifetime, able to find a way out. Macondo is founded, and during the journey, Úrsula gives birth to their first son, José Arcadio, who is tail-free. Nonetheless, the curse of a pig's tail lingers throughout Macondo's history. Any other Buendía who mates with anyone with of the same blood, it is said, will suffer a child showing the mark of incest. The theme of incest remains prevalent throughout *One Hundred Years of Solitude*. Macondo, and the Buendía family, will be founded on and eventually destroyed by incest. It can be argued that mankind in Genesis is engendered by incest, if we consider that Eve, made from Adam's rib, is more genetically related to him than an actual sister. In both the Bible and Greek myth, incest often yields tragedy.

José Arcadio is the first infant to bless Macondo's founding; he is immediately followed by Aureliano Buendía, the future Colonel. They will also have a younger sister, Amaranta. Chapter 2 is devoted to the oldest brother, José Arcadio, and his coming of age. He has a simple mind, and his lack of intellectual curiosity makes his relationship with his father fraught. From the first, José Arcadio seems to be distinguished by nothing but his enormous physique and his equally impressive, and terrifying, sexual endowment. "My boy," one woman exclaims upon seeing him, "may God preserve you just the way you are."

Úrsula is terrified that a penis the size of her son's is as grotesque an attribute as a pig's tail, and she consults the local fortune teller, Pilar Ternera. Ternera, aroused by Úrsula's tales, goes to check—thoroughly—the truth of the matter, and does not find herself disappointed. Shortly afterward, José Arcadio comes to her hammock, and in their tussle, his awkward, adolescent feelings vanish. They become lovers, with the result that Pilar Ternera becomes pregnant with José Arcadio's son. Then during Pilar Ternera's pregnancy, José Arcadio tumbles into bed with a young gypsy girl. Two days later, he ties a red scarf around his head, gypsy style, and follows her band of wanderers when they leave town.

Pilar Ternera is in many ways like the gypsies, for she tempts the Buendía clan. But the gypsies come and go as they please, while Ternera—a founding Macondo member—and the village are inextricably linked. A woman desperately in love with the man that raped her when she was fourteen, she fled from that love and ended up in Macondo. She has a smoky scent, and an infectious laugh that sounds like glass shattering and that—symbolic of her sinful role—frightens the doves away. José Arcadio's son is only the first Buendía son that she will illegitimately mother; she will go on to give birth to another, and orchestrate the siring of many others. Her primary influence, therefore, is more biological than intellectual, and probably essential for the perpetuation of the Buendía line, for if it were not for her, they would continue to propagate among themselves. But like the gypsies she also has magic—for she is talented in the art of Tarot reading, and throughout the story, the Buendías consult her and act according to what she predicts. The gypsies bring the future into Macondo through their inventions. Pilar Ternera brings it to the village with her womb and her cards.

While José Arcadio is still in town frolicking with Pilar Ternera, a third child, Amaranta, is born to Úrsula. Soon afterward, José Arcadio leaves town. His father is not bothered by the disappearance of his oldest son, with whom he has no empathy. But Úrsula, only just recovered from the birth of her daughter, sets out in pursuit. More than five months pass before she returns. She has not found her son, but she has found towns with commerce and a regular postal system. She has, in short, found a route out of Macondo, and the first break in Macondo's solitude is made.

With a mail system and a major road, Macondo becomes a boom town, bustling with shops and newcomers; this is the situation at **chapter 3.** José Arcadio Buendía plants almond trees along the roadsides and makes the streets sing with musical clocks that he has installed in every house. Pilar Ternera gives birth to José Arcadio's son, who is baptized José Arcadio and taken into the Buendía household to be raised with Amaranta. Úrsula begins a profitable business selling candy animals and hires servants to take care of the children.

Now a teenager, Úrsula's second son, Aureliano Buendía, takes over his father's laboratory. Aureliano, who will grow up to be the same Colonel in the book's opening lines, is serious where his elder brother was rambunctious, and is said to have wept in his mother's womb. He and his older brother are first of a series of José Arcadios and Aurelianos, all marked with the same characteristics. Many years and chapters later, Úrsula will observe:

> While the Aurelianos were withdrawn, but with
> lucid minds, the José Arcadios were impulsive and

enterprising, but they were marked with a tragic sign.

The first Aureliano Buendía is born with his eyes open, (a sign of his clear-mindedness and foresight) and will keep them open for the rest of his life. All in all, he is a lucid, somber boy. He shares his father's fascination with the wonders of science; hence, it is Aureliano whom his father takes to see the ice. Preferring solitude to the company of others, he shuts himself in the laboratory and teaches himself metal work. Aureliano also has a gift for premonition; he knows when a pot of soup will spill, that Pilar Ternera has been sleeping with his brother, and announces the arrival of the last addition to his generation, an orphan girl named Rebeca.

Rebeca is thin, hungry, silent. She sucks her thumb and bears, amongst other things, a sack containing the bones of her parents, which go *cloc-cloc*. No one knows where she comes from. She has a tendency to eat dirt—mud from the courtyard, limestone from the walls, earthworms, and snails. When Úrsula finally whips her out of the habit, Rebeca becomes a normal, well-behaved girl; she plays with the other children and is equally fluent in Spanish and the indigenous language, and the household accepts her as a Buendía. Unfortunately, sometime in her mysterious past life, Rebeca was infected with the plague of insomnia. It does not exhibit itself until much later, when she is discovered rocking the night away in her chair with her eyes aglow. Before long, the entire household is contaminated, and then, thanks to the lucrative candy business that Úrsula runs out of the house, sleeplessness takes over the town. At first the inhabitants are delighted, for insomnia multiplies their productivity. But then they succumb to its more dangerous side effect—memory loss. Soon, they are posting signs to remind themselves of the names of things and their use: "This is the cow. She must be milked every morning so that she will produce milk, and milk must be boiled in order to be mixed with coffee to make coffee and milk." The loss of names leads to the loss of thoughts and feelings; eventually, they are unable to recognize their mothers and fathers, and need a sign to remind them that "GOD EXISTS." Days pass without meaning. Since they have quarantined themselves from the neighboring communities, they are a ghost town. In a town where the future *is* the past, progress vanishes with memory.

Melquíades arrives; finding the solitude of death unbearable, he has brought himself back to life. Among other things, he has a daguerreotype for photographing things to remember in days to come (a handy invention for insomniacs and the first invention of Melquíades that Úrsula is keen to use). Even more helpfully, he has a potion to cure them all. Once again, it is an outsider who saves Macondo from its self-inflicted solitude. Life, reality, and technological advancement resume.

With it resumes the maturation of the Buendía children. Aureliano becomes an expert silversmith; he also leaves his workshop to be deflowered by a gypsy girl, whose sexual services are pimped by her enormously fat grandmother. (The exploits of this gypsy girl are continued in the García Márquez short story "The Tale of Innocent Erendira and Her Cruel Grandmother") The girls Rebeca and Amaranta have also blossomed. Úrsula realizes that it is time to introduce them as young women into the world; and with the education of her daughters and the future in mind, she expands the house to the proportions of a small castle, with baths, a rose garden, a formal parlor, a two-oven kitchen, and an aviary where birds could roost at will.

Another visitor arrives, a man by the name of Don Apolinar Moscote whom the government has appointed as magistrate. Moscote is timid and elegant man, and José Arcadio despises him immediately. Moscote's first order is for all the village houses to be painted the Conservative color blue, and, enraged, José Arcadio Buendía drives him out. Moscote responds by returning with soldiers, and José Arcadio Buendía has no choice but to let him settle (although the colors of the houses stay the same). The new magistrate brings with him a wife and seven daughters, the youngest of whom is nine years old, lily-white and green-eyed, and named Remedios, and who sends daggers and daydreams into Aureliano Buendía's heart.

While José Arcadio Buendía dreams of the world abroad, Úrsula imports it. **Chapter 4** finds her furnishing her house with crystal from Bohemia and furniture from Vienna, and lamps and drapes from all over the world. She inaugurates the new house with a dance—again, tailored for her newly adult daughters—and hires a blond Italian called Pietro Crespi to tune her new Italian pianola, and to teach Rebeca and Amaranta how to dance to the latest songs.

The house, in García Márquez's words, is "full of love." Aureliano dreams of Remedios, the Moscote daughter, who at nine years of age "still wets her bed." He writes endless reams of poetry about her, and gives her a little gold fish that he himself has forged. Meanwhile, both girls (despite their father's assertion that Pietro Crespi is a homosexual) are in love with their handsome instructor. Rebeca's love is requited, with Crespi's love notes and dried flowers and pressed butterflies. Amaranta, who is the less beautiful of the two girls, loves Crespi to no avail, and her jealousy of Rebeca engenders a Cain-and-Abel situation that will only grow more angry and violent with time. For Amaranta has rancor in her bones, and this seemingly frivolous love-squabble is the first chance it has had to manifest itself. Rebeca, who must keep her affair with Crespi secret, is driven back to her old habit of consuming dirt. She chips her teeth on snail shells, chews earthworms, and vomits until she is unconscious. Úrsula discovers the affair and, alarmed, agrees to allow the lovers to marry, especially considering that Pietro Crespi plans to open a lucrative business selling musical knick-knacks with his brother, Bruno. Pilar Ternera, who has changed brothers and is now Aureliano Buendía's mistress, makes wedding arrangements for her lover and Remedios. A satisfactory conclusion has been reached for all, it would seem, except for the fact that Amaranta threatens repeatedly to kill Rebeca and, no matter how her new fiancé tries to distract her with mechanical ballerinas, music boxes, and sprigs of lavender, Rebeca truly fears for her life.

In the meantime, Melquíades dies—for the second time. Sharing a workshop with Aureliano, he spends his last few months scribbling indecipherable phrases on parchment that crumples "like puff paste." He loses his appetite, he forgets to put in the false teeth that once made him so youthful, and his skin is covered with moss. "I have found immortality," he proclaims to José Arcadio Buendía, and when he is found drowned in the river, José Arcadio Buendía burns mercury in his death-room for three days (per Melquíades' request) in a futile hope of resurrecting him. Melquíades' death is the first in Macondo. Just as he has brought Macondo wisdom, so too he brings to this Edenic village the taint that is a mortal life.

With Melquíades gone, Pilar Ternera is the only soothsayer remaining. She predicts that Rebeca will never be happy until she has buried her parents' bones; Rebeca, unaware of her parentage, is baffled. (Úrsula overhears and searches madly; finally she consults the contractors she hired to reconstruct the house and finds that one of them, annoyed by the bones' noise, immured them. Úrsula finds the bones and buries them in secrecy.) But it is Pilar Ternera's prediction for Aureliano Buendía that is the clearest and perhaps the most damning. She leaves him the legacy that will sculpt the rest of his life: "You'd be good in war," she tells him, "Where you put your eye, you will put your bullet."

The end of chapter four is devoted to José Arcadio Buendía's disintegration. José Arcadio Buendía is the original man, founding both a clan and a town with both his delusion and determination. Melquíades was the figure who showed him that everything was possible. With Melquíades dies the promise that has driven this patriarch most of his life, and now José Arcadio Buendía has lost his faith. With no hope for the future, José Arcadio Buendía retreats into the past, in this case by rekindling a friendship with the ghost of Prudencio Aguilar—whom he killed so many years ago with a spear, and whose death drove José Arcadio Buendía out of his own hometown. José Arcadio Buendía becomes convinced that every day is a repeat of the day before; he spends hours looking for proof that some change has occurred in the last twenty-four hours, and finding none, loses his mind. As has often been suggested, there never has been progress in Macondo, because everything operates on a loop; in his insanity José Arcadio has actually hit upon the truth, and the resulting madness is that of a man attempting to decipher something linear in the circular Macondo world. He also finds himself unable to speak anything but Latin, which to everyone else is incomprehensible babble. Insanity, therefore, is relative; in any other world, a man who speaks the pure language of the Church and who pursues linear progress would be its sanest and wisest member; in Macondo he is mad. José Arcadio Buendía's sons and his twenty-odd neighbors (for the patriarch is a physical monster, broad-shouldered and gigantic) drag him to the chestnut tree in the courtyard, tie him to it, and leave him there to spend the end of his days.

Chapter 5 commences with Remedios' first menstrual period. Remedios, who, since the conclusion of the marriage negotiations, has been educated by the Buendía family, is finally woman enough to exchange vows with Aureliano Buendía. The occasion is unhappy for Rebeca, however, who was to exchange her vows with Crespi the same day, only to have Crespi receive a telegram informing him of his mother's impending death. Post-marriage, Crespi returns, having found his mother in a perfectly healthy state.

Remedios, the new bride barely out of infancy in her pink organza and white boots, is a joy, perhaps the most undiluted sweetness that the Buendía family will ever know. At her wedding, she cuts off the largest piece of wedding cake to feed to her mad father-in-law—José Arcadio Buendía—and after her marriage she takes charge of washing the nits from his beard. When Pilar Ternera's child by Aureliano Buendía (baptized Aureliano José) is brought into the household, she welcomes it as a child of her own. "Her merry vitality," García Márquez writes, "... went like a whirlwind of good health along the porch with the begonias." Remedios' brightness is infectious. Because of his child-wife, Aureliano strikes up a friendship with his father-in-law, the magistrate Don Apolinar Moscote, consolidating Moscote's authority and allowing policemen to patrol the streets.

Meanwhile, Macondo's new priest, Father Nicanor Reyna, entertains the town with his ability to float in the air while holding cups of hot chocolate. He dreams of converting all of Macondo's inhabitants, and also of building the biggest church in the world. Nicanor becomes the new friend of José Arcadio Buendía—still tied to the chestnut tree—because he is the only man who recognizes Buendía's rants as Latin, and the two of them sit under the chestnut tree, play checkers, and dispute the existence of God. Meanwhile, Rebeca and Crespi's union has been indefinitely postponed for the completion of Father Nicanor's lunatic project so that their marriage can be the first ceremony to inaugurate his new church (a suggestion of Amaranta's). Crespi is too timid to elope, and Rebeca smolders with sexual frustration. Úrsula surprises her adopted daughter exchanging kisses on her lover's lap. Desperate, Crespi gives the priest the money he needs to complete the church.

Amaranta, whose rage toward her sister has only seasoned with time, becomes disturbed with what she perceives as her deadline. She removes the mothballs from Rebeca's wedding dress, so that when Rebeca unfolds it days later, it disintegrates into shreds—a foreshadowing of Amaranta's later practice of unweaving her own shroud. Amaranta vows to poison her adopted sister with laudanum in her coffee. She prays for something horrible to happen to prevent the wedding. That tragedy occurs; for Remedios dies, with twin fetuses entwined in her belly.

Even Amaranta is repentant. Úrsula orders a year of silence, and the daguerreotype of Remedios with a ribbon around her hair to be set up as an altar with an oil lamp forever burning. Aureliano's son by Pilar Ternera—Aureliano José—who was adopted by Remedios is now handed over to the care of Amaranta. Rebeca and Pietro Crespi's wedding is once again postponed.

Then one day an enormous man pushes his way through the door, every inch of him covered in tattoos. "His skin was tanned by the salt of the open air, his hair was short and straight like a mule, his jaws were of iron, and he wore a sad smile." He is the missing José Arcadio, oldest son of José Arcadio Buendía and Úrsula, who now has been around the world sixty-five times. True to his enterprising nature, he sets up a business auctioning off his enormous manhood for ten pesos a woman. Most of the family is repulsed by his monster belches and farts, but Rebeca is attracted. One day she comes to him as he dwells in his hammock, he runs his fingers up her thighs, and the heat that has been simmering during her long engagement with Crespi finally explodes. Three days later they are married.

This is incest, but not in the truest sense, for Rebeca is a Buendía by nature and name, but not by blood. The couple themselves, however, are not aware of this, for Rebeca came to the Buendías after José Arcadio's departure. "She's your sister," protests Pietro Crespi, to which José Arcadio retorts, "I don't care." Perhaps it is because of the deliberate flouting of the incest taboo that Úrsula—the only member of the family who knows that the two are not related—forbid the newlyweds from ever entering her house. The couple move to a house across from the cemetery, furnished with nothing but José Arcadio's hammock, and the entire town is kept awake by their passionate yowls. "You will be happy," José Arcadio Buendía told Rebeca when she first buried her parents bones. He was correct, but what he did not foresee was with whom she would find that contentment.

Now a widower, Aureliano Buendía throws himself into politics. The conflict between the Conservatives (of whom Aureliano's father-in-law, Don Moscote, is one representative) and the Liberals has intensified. Liberals are pro–civil unions and for the legitimization of illegitimate children. The Conservatives, on the other hand, are against anything that is not sanctioned by the Church. Both sides itch for war. In part because of his loyalty to his father-in-law, Aureliano's allegiances are undecided—that is until Aureliano sees Moscote tamper with the local election ballots. Shocked, Aureliano turns to the Liberals, only to make the acquaintance of a doctor whose solution to the political problem is a mass-poisoning of the other side. This is a point that García Márquez will repeatedly emphasize throughout his book—that despite their stated differences, the Liberals and Conservatives are equally crazed, equally complicit. Civil war is declared, with horrific aftermath. Conservative soldiers assassinate civilians without trial, shoot the doctor, split the priest's head open with a rifle butt, and beat to death a woman bitten by a mad dog. Aureliano Buendía chooses the Liberal side, but essentially his decision is based on timing. The moment he is forced to pick one out of two undesirable parties is the exact instant that the Conservatives behave the most atrociously. Aureliano shoulders his gun and prepares to fulfill the destiny that Pilar Ternera told him of years ago: "Get the boys ready," he tells his friend Gerineldo Márquez. "We're going to war." That night Márquez, Aureliano, and thirty other men execute the Conservative captain and retake Macondo for the Liberals. Thus Aureliano Buendía the civilian ceases; Aureliano Buendía the legendary Colonel is born.

SECTION II: Chapters 6–9

The start of section two, **chapter 6** finds García Márquez indulging in what is now to us a familiar narrative trick—yet another glimpse into Colonel Aureliano's future:

Colonel Aureliano Buendía organized thirty-two armed uprisings and he lost them all. He had seventeen male children by seventeen different women.... He survived fourteen attempts on his life, seventy-three ambushes, and a firing squad. He lived through a dose of strychnine in his coffee that was enough to kill a horse.

He will also refuse governmental honors, be instrumental in the peace treaty of Neerlandia, and retire to his metal shop to while away the rest of his days. By the time the section concludes, he will have accomplished what is promised in these first opening lines.

For now, however, we return to the start of Colonel Aureliano Buendía's career and the onset of the war. Also, Melquíades has returned to Macondo in phantom form. As a ghost, he is more powerful than Melquíades as a human man. Dying has made him divine. In the end, Melquíades has fulfilled his promise to José Arcadio Buendía and become immortal. The first time Melquíades died, death was still too lonely. By the time he dies for the second time, he has made peace with eternal solitude, and hence transcends his human self to climb to more exalted echelons. Michael Bell calls him a combination of "trickster" and "necessarily lonely Creator." (Bell, 68) Melquíades as a ghost is now more than Macondo's prophet and tempter, he is Macondo's God.

Melquíades befriends Arcadio, the illegitimate child of Pilar Ternera and José Arcadio. An outcast throughout most of his life, and teased for the feminine shape of his buttocks, Arcadio spends most of his childhood locked in the old workshop—the first Buendía to attempt to decipher the gypsy's manuscripts. When Aureliano Buendía marches off to war, he leaves his nephew Arcadio in charge. Immediately, Arcadio abandons his intellectual pursuits for the flashier trappings of command. In moments, Arcadio abandons what one might call the introverted "Aureliano" aspects of his character and fulfills the foolhardy, lusty characteristics that his name Arcadio promises. As the new Liberal leader of Macondo, Arcadio dons a gold-braided uniform, imprisons the local clergy, orders random executions, enforces the mandatory wearing of red armbands, and, as the final insult to the Conservatives, flogs the Moscote daughters and orders the execution of his in-law Don Moscote, to whom Aureliano has promised protection. Úrsula, exasperated, saves the Moscote family, reinstitutes Sunday mass and frees those whom Arcadio has taken prisoner. Despite her victory, Úrsula is miserable. Her husband is a lunatic tied to a chestnut tree. Her grandson is a monster. Her son and her daughter are frolicking in an incestuous marriage, and she has banned them from her sight. So she sits with her mad husband and distracts him with a string of lies.

The rest of the Buendías are doing better than their mother. Despite their exile, Rebeca and José Arcadio are extraordinarily happy in their marriage. Their cottage is a sunlit, well-scrubbed refuge; José Arcadio ceases to be a layabout and now uses his strength to plow fields and hunt wild ducks and rabbits for dinner. Amaranta is being courted by Pietro Crespi, whose business in mechanical music knick-knacks is booming. With the sister he once spurned, Pietro Crespi is finding a love that is more to his taste—less lusty, less jolting—hours on the veranda translating Petrarchan sonnets and embroidering. When Arcadio becomes infatuated with Pilar Ternera, unaware that she is his actual mother (it makes him the only Buendía with an Oedipal complex) Pilar Ternera diverts him to the arms of Santa Sofía de la Piedad—a twenty-year-old virgin who sells her purity for 50 pesos, and who smells of flower lotion, with "blind breasts" and eyelashes so endless "they looked as though they were artificial." They move in together. She bears him twins, José Arcadio Segundo and Aureliano Segundo, and promptly becomes pregnant again.

The bliss is only temporary. When Pietro Crespi declares to Amaranta that they will be married, she scorns him. "Don't be simple, Crespi," she tells him, "I wouldn't marry you even if I were dead." Her youthful resentment has made her incapable of loving even the man who sparked her jealousy in the first place. Spurned by two sisters, Pietro Crespi commits suicide by slitting his wrists in his shop. In a moment of remorse, Amaranta burns her hand. She wears a black gauze bandage to cover the scar; but when the scar is healed and Pietro Crespi is long forgotten, the bandage will stay wrapped around her wrist as a symbol of the perpetual loneliness that will follow her to the grave. In the meantime, the town of Macondo falls to the Conservatives. Arcadio is shot against the cemetery wall, and expires with "Long live the Liberal Party!" on his lips. He leaves behind the legacy of a political bully, a pregnant mistress with twins to raise, and no one to much miss him except Pilar Ternera, the mother he never knew he had.

Aureliano Buendía is captured abroad but brought back to Macondo for execution. **Chapter 7** brings us back to the opening sentence, as he prepares to face the firing squad. Úrsula manages to bully her way into his prison cell, taking with her candy and clean clothes for her condemned son. "What did you expect?" she sighs, "Time passes." "That's how it goes," he replies, "but not so much." Aureliano gives Úrsula his poetry to Remedios to burn, but she holds off. Something tells her that her son may yet escape. Aureliano Buendía himself is not entirely convinced of his impending death. His foresight—that once marked his childhood and has since helped him stave off numerous assassination attempts—seems to tell him that he has years left. On the appointed day and time, the Colonel is marched out into the courtyard, blindfolded, and he arranges himself in the position in which we found him at the start of the book—in front of the firing squad. Just as the order is given to shoot, José Arcadio strides into the courtyard, points his rifle at the soldiers, and forces the execution to be called off. With this one miraculous escape, the myth that is Colonel Aureliano Buendía begins. Wildly conflicting rumors will circulate as to his whereabouts. He is dead in a swamp, he is eaten by Indians, he is always magically resurrected and is fighting in several parts of the country at once. Aurelianos, traditionally, are not destined for a violent death, but Colonel Aureliano pushes this to an extreme; after all, after the firing squad, he survives "fourteen attempts on his life," "a dose strychnine," and a bullet that he put in his own chest. No matter how fatal the situation he is in, he is impossible to kill.

A new war breaks out. The captain assigned to execute Aureliano Buendía, Captain Roque Carnicero, joins Aureliano as they embark on a new military campaign. Aureliano Buendía communicates sporadically with his family and with his friend General Márquez (who is still technically a Conservative hostage) through the newly opened telegraph office.

Santa Sofía de la Piedad gives birth to a daughter, whom Úrsula names Remedios, and she and her three children install themselves into the Buendía household. José Arcadio comes home one day with a brace of rabbits for dinner, shuts himself in his bedroom, and ends up with a bullet in his head. The blood creeps out of the bedroom, through the town, and into the Buendía house, where it avoids the carpet, and trickles into the kitchen, where Úrsula is baking bread. Úrsula discovers her son's body by following the umbilical cord–like trail. The circumstances of José Arcadio's death are mysterious; the couple have been too happy together to explain why he might have committed suicide or why his wife, Rebeca, the only other person in the house at the time, might have wanted to murder him. Not surprisingly then, José Arcadio's death is a restless one. The smell of gunpowder lingers on his body; his family tries to scrub it off with soap, lye, and chemicals. They contemplate boiling it with herbs before decomposition forces them to bury the body in a coffin sealed with iron; for years later, the cemetery will smell of powder. Rebeca also buries herself, in her house—she seals the doors and windows and goes out only once more in her long life.

The Liberals are victorious, and Colonel Aureliano Buendía marches home, boots out the Conservatives, and installs himself as leader. He is physically indolent but tormented, as he realizes with increasing clarity that he fights not for love, politics, or ideals, but for pride alone. One day he ingests strychnine-laced coffee. The brush with death revives him; as soon as he can walk, he goes back to battle, leaving his close friend Colonel Gerineldo Márquez in charge.

The Buendías receive one important communication from the Colonel after he departs. "Take good care of Papa," his telegram reads, "because he is going to die." José Arcadio Buendía has been dead to the world for many years now. His only companion is a ghost—Prudencio Aguilar. It takes seven men to carry him into his bedroom. And despite the guilt his family feels for having forgotten him, José Arcadio Buendía still dies alone. Indeed, his passing goes unnoticed. Indeed, the family must be informed of his passing by an outside messenger—an Indian family servant who has long since fled Macondo and who now returns dressed in an enormous black hat and looks like Melquíades. "I have come," he says, "for the exequies of the king." And when they go to check on him, they find that, indeed, their king is dead. Yellow blossoms fall from the sky, smothering animals and compacting the streets, and the next morning they have to clear them with rakes so the funeral procession can pass.

Amaranta Buendía may live her life a sour virgin, but she is not without her suitors. Besides Pietro Crespi, Colonel Gerineldo Márquez has been in love with her as long as he can remember. There are also the incestuous urgings that she inspires. When we meet Aureliano José in **chapter 8** he is already half-grown, with a mustache and a passion for his aunt, the virgin Amaranta, who brought him up. Since he was a boy he has woken up regularly in her bed. As he grows up, friendly aunt-nephew caresses become playful love tussles—they chase each other and play kissing games until Amaranta realizes what she is doing and cuts off contact. Aureliano José attempts to defuse his frustration in military maneuvers. As do most heartbroken lads, he joins Macondo's Liberal army.

Once again, Macondo falls to the Conservatives. Colonel Márquez and Aureliano José are among the men who flee with the aid of Aureliano Buendía. The new Conservative leader is General Moncada, and under him, the town blossoms. Moncada is a gentle man who wears civilian clothes, who keeps Úrsula company while she knits in the evenings. Macondo now boasts an open-air theatre and a renovated school for its children. Moncada also knows Aureliano and respects him, for they have played checkers in their brief respites from war, and will eventually be the godfather to one of Aureliano's many sons. For it is around this time that Aureliano's seventeen offspring from seventeen women—the result of a custom of sending daughters to successful military leaders for the night—start showing up on the Buendía doorstep to be baptized, all of them with the name Aureliano. There are mulatto Aurelianos, muscular Aurelianos, even an Aureliano with hair like a girl who asks for the mechanical ballerina that Pietro Crespi gave Rebeca so long ago.

As soon as he hears that it is legal to marry ones aunt, Aureliano José deserts the army and comes home. Nights he spends creeping into her bed with nothing on, with her resisting, repeating the family curse that their boys will have pig's tails. "I don't care if they're born as armadillos," he replies, unknowingly echoing his own grandfather years ago when he forced himself upon Úrsula. Then one night Amaranta locks the door on Aureliano José once and for all. Her nephew finds comfort in debauchery, which he finds at the establishment run by his natural mother, Pilar Ternera. Pilar

Ternera, in her old age, can no longer deliver sexual condolence with her own body, so she provides it in other ways. Her house is now a hothouse dedicated to the cultivation of passion—she lends her bed for liaisons, fixes up young lovers, and charges nothing for the service. The night he dies, Aureliano José is destined to meet his true love Carmelita Montiel, a twenty-year-old virgin, a girl similar to Santa Sofía de la Piedad, whom Pilar Ternera introduced to Arcadio. Unfortunately, Aureliano José goes out into the streets after curfew, and is shot in the back by Conservative soldiers. It is a death that was not meant to be—a mistake in the cards. For years, Pilar Ternera has read a full future for her second son, and that night only, the cards were tricked, and Aureliano José takes a bullet meant for another man. In taking it Aureliano José—contrary to the promise of his Aureliano name—meets a sudden end.

Colonel Aureliano Buendía storms into Macondo. Conservative soldiers are executed. The Liberals are victorious. The last court martial that Aureliano Buendía orders is for the Colonel's old friend General Moncada, who is sentenced to death. Aureliano Buendía tells his friend. "Remember, old friend. I'm not shooting you. It's the revolution that's shooting you." Revolution has made a monster out of the Colonel, who cares no longer for old loyalties or even for his family. Unfortunately, the revolution for which the Colonel has sacrificed his compassion is a mockery. The conflicting parties have become comic in their sameness—as madcap as Alice in Wonderland's squabbling twins Tweedledum and Tweedledee, who "decided to have a battle / Said Tweedledum to Tweedledee, you have spoilt my nice new rattle." Macondo, indeed, is as politically worthless as any baby's toy. Its ownership is only crucial to a handful of narcissists.

The wiser members of Aureliano Buendía's troupe are aware of this. "All we're fighting for," Colonel Márquez complains at the beginning of **chapter 9**, "is power." Colonel Aureliano Buendía agrees with the general, but it does not bother him—it has been some time since he stopped convincing himself that he was fighting for ideals. Meanwhile, political turmoil has reached an impasse. Colonel Aureliano has three concubines, a hammock, and the title of leader of the rebels. But life without war is inconceivable. Because of the absence of war, he has the luxury to realize that he has loved nothing in his life—not his family, not even Remedios. "Watch out for your heart," Colonel Márquez tells him, "You're rotting alive." He has become a stranger, even to Úrsula. "I'm sorry," he tells her, "it's just that the war has done away with everything."

So he burns the love poetry that he wrote to Remedios and that Úrsula preserved, signs an armistice with the Colombian government, and shoots himself in the chest. But Aureliano Buendía cannot be killed by a bullet—he is destined for a quiet end. During his recovery, a military guard is posted outside his house. By the time Aureliano can walk again, his conspirators are either dead, assimilated, or exiled. Úrsula refuses to be beaten down by her son's depression. She restores the house to its past splendor and enlists the help of the troops outside the house. The pianola sings; the walls are whitewashed. Life returns to the way it was when Rebeca and Amaranta were young women—unknowingly, Úrsula has also resurrected the old passions, ferment, and loneliness. Aureliano returns to his workshop to hammer out his little gold fishes, and Amaranta's rancor is as renewed as when Pietro Crespi spurned her. Longing runs as fresh as before. And on New Year's Day, the commander of the troops guarding the Buendía house shoots himself for a girl called Remedios the Beauty, the daughter of dead Arcadio and Santa Sofía de la Piedad.

SECTION III: Chapters 10–14

"Years later on his deathbed, Aureliano Segundo would remember the rainy afternoon in June when he went into the bedroom to meet his first son." So **chapter 10**, which marks the novel's halfway point, begins, with the deathbed recollections of another Aureliano. Just as Aureliano Buendía remembered ice as he stood in front of the firing squad, so Aureliano Segundo chooses to relive the moment he decided to call his child José Arcadio.

Aureliano Segundo and his brother José Arcadio Segundo are twin sons of the deceased Arcadio and his young girl mistress, Santa Sofía de la Piedad, who has taken up residence with the Buendía family. As boys, the twins are giddy and identical. Úrsula, who is already a hundred years old, makes them wear different-colored shirts and armbands to distinguish them. Mischievous, the boys switch shirts and throw the family—and their teachers and other town civilians—into a muddle. But the similarity does not end with the physical; the twins are synchronized beings. They go to the bathroom at the same time; they are susceptible to the same diseases. One twin drinks a glass of lemonade, and just as he takes the first sip, the other announces that it doesn't have sugar. It is only in adulthood that they grow apart. But even this is strange, for the twins exhibit the traits of the opposite namesakes—Aureliano starts to behave like a José Arcadio and vice versa—leading Úrsula to suspect that sometime in their childhood, they switched identities and didn't switch back.

At first Aureliano Segundo does exhibit certain "aurelianic" traits. Driven by academic curiosity, he retires to the old chamber formerly inhabited by Melquíades, and he spends many hours studying historical texts under the tutelage of Melquíades' ghost, but he keeps his relationship with the gypsy secret. He tries to teach himself metalworking but is not skilled like the Colonel. He also pores over the gypsy's mysterious parchments, even though Melquíades says they will not be read until they have reached one hundred years of age. Perhaps the one man he most resembles in these adolescent years is the original José Arcadio Buendía. "That's what your great-grandfather did," Úrsula says when she overhears him with Melquíades in the study, "He used to talk to himself as well."

As he matures, Aureliano Segundo develops a gigantic physique and a tendency toward dissipation, in contrast to his brother, José Arcadio Segundo, who is dark, bony, and serious. Nevertheless, the twins are still enough alike to share an unwitting mistress—the sleek, gold-eyed and beautiful Petra Cotes. Eventually, José Arcadio Segundo drops out. Aureliano Segundo abandons Melquíades' study—along with his attempts toward scholarship and metalwork—for more immediate pleasures. With Petra Cotes, Aureliano Segundo proves that he has not only inherited the arcadian physique, but also the arcadian libido.

Petra Cotes raffles livestock for a living. To the scandal of Úrsula, Aureliano Segundo moves in with Petra Cotes, and the two embark on a business more fecund than in their wildest dreams. For all of Cotes and Aureliano Segundo's copulation, they never have children of their own; their sexual activity is manifested in the animals that they raise. They begin with raffling rabbits; when the rabbits overtake the yard, they trade them in for cattle, which immediately begin bearing triplets. Their profits reproduce at the same rate. Aureliano Segundo papers the Buendía mansion with one-peso notes, and then a plaster saint filled with gold coins is uncovered in the house. Úrsula, who once made candies to ensure her family could eat, is horrified by the extravagance. Their fortune is turning in circles—this time, lucratively. No matter how hard the Buendías now try to spend money, it returns with abundance. Aureliano Buendía is caught in his own circle—albeit a less profitable one. He hammers out so many gold fishes that he essentially takes the gold coins he gets in payment and transforms them back into fishes. But the family is flailing in so much wealth that this does not present a problem.

The family fortune gives Aureliano Segundo's twin an opportunity to make something of himself. José Arcadio Segundo has been less successful in life than his brother. As a child, he witnessed an execution, and was horrified to see the condemned man buried while still twitching. For the rest of his life, the fear of being buried alive will haunt him. He tries religion and scholarship, but to no avail—he seems to exhibit neither extraordinary intellect, nor sensuality, nor business sense. (Úrsula considers him "the quietest example" that the family has ever produced.) Ultimately, his young manhood is spent breeding fighting cocks at the home of Pilar Ternera. With the newly acquired Buendía wealth, José Arcadio Segundo pursues yet another age-old family obsession—

exploration. He is convinced that he can find a route to the sea. Though Úrsula has always viewed such excursions as reckless, the family can afford it. Eventually José Arcadio Segundo digs a canal, sets off in a log raft, and returns on that same raft, with a flock of cultivated (and painted) ladies from France.

These French ladies deck the streets with Japanese lanterns and educate the villagers in the modern, continental ways of sex. Eventually, they propose a carnival, and Remedios the Beauty, younger sister of the twins, is the only choice for the carnival queen. Remedios the Beauty has looks that kill and a maddening scent—quite possibly the most alluring young woman in the world. She has already caused the death of one young man, a commander who shot himself under her window. Úrsula will take her out in public only if she has a veil over her face. One foreign gentleman gives her a rose in church; she lifts the veil to give him a smile of thanks and leaves most of the Macondo men insane—and the profferer of the rose doomed to wander the world in rags and be cut to pieces, many years later, by a train.

Remedios is also simple-minded; for if José Arcadios are lusty and Aurelianos are introspective, then Remedios Buendías are lovely, happy, and simple. She paints little animals on the wall with her excrement, cannot use utensils at the dinner table, and walks around in the nude for comfort. Naturally, she has no understanding of the men that die for her—she thinks that they are fools. "See how simple he is," she announces over the body of the young commander that shoots himself, "he says that's he's dying because of me, as if it was a bad case of colic...a complete simpleton." Sharp-sighted Colonel Aureliano Buendía asserts that she is not mentally challenged, but infinitely wise.

Decked out in ermine, Remedios sails through the town, only to be met by a parade of pretenders with their own queen, a girl named Fernanda del Carpio. Shots ring out to the chorus of "Long live the Liberal Party"; the imposters are massacred, and their queen, spattered in blood, is nursed back to health by Úrsula. After Fernanda leaves to return home, Aureliano Segundo follows her into the jungle. He tracks her, finds her, and brings her back to Macondo, where he marries her in a festival that lasts for twenty days.

Petra Cotes, Aureliano Segundo's lifelong mistress, is not disturbed by her lover's marriage. **Chapter 11** provides us with a more thorough portrait of his new bride. It turns out that Fernanda is not only a bewitching beauty and former imposter queen, she is also a true highlander, by tradition pompous and archaic. Raised believing she would be the queen of Madagascar, she was educated in piano, Latin poetry, and the more sophisticated discourses on God, and had no contact with the world until puberty. She eats from silver table service, uses a golden chamber pot that bears her family crest, weaves funeral wreaths to earn a living, and speaks in an affected, euphemistic speech that no one can quite understand. After the Carnival bloodbath, she retreats to her home village, locks herself in her room, and stays there until Aureliano Segundo manages to coax her out.

From the start, their marriage is unpromising. The wedding celebrations last for twenty days because Fernanda is unwilling to surrender her virginity; when she finally does, she does it in a nightgown with a strategically positioned slit. Despite the fact that Aureliano Segundo and Fernanda produce three children through these comically precious nightly rituals—"I should have married a Sister of Charity," scoffs Aureliano Segundo—it is no surprise that Aureliano Segundo finds himself once more in the bed of Petra Cotes, where their numerous consummations result in more rabbits, more cattle, and no children at all. Fernanda agrees to this arrangement with one condition: that at the end, her husband should not die in Petra's bed.

Perhaps in frustration, Fernanda takes over command of the Buendía house, redecorating it with the royal, religious style to which she is accustomed—upholstery, glaring marble statues, mealtimes with linen and silver. She bans the pastry and candy business that has kept the Buendía family afloat, deeming it beneath her dignity. She and Amaranta cease speaking and communicate about household affairs in notes. Úrsula, who was appalled by the decadence of Petra Cotes, is even more alarmed by the bizarre and morbid formality imposed by Fernanda. The bedrooms of Aureliano Segundo's children are crowded with statues of saints, made lifelike by glass eyes; their mother lectures them on the virtues of grandparents they have never met. (One Christmas, Don Fernando—Fernanda's father—sends them his own preserved corpse in a trunk.) Fernanda's holy behavior sparks in Úrsula perhaps the first glimmer of mischief Úrsula has ever had. The seventeen sons of Aureliano Buendía return, all of them named after their father; they are lusty brutes. "The three days that they stayed in the house, to the scandal of Fernanda and the satisfaction of Úrsula, were like a state of war." They break dishes; they cheeringly persuade Remedios the Beauty to climb a greased pole. Colonel Aureliano, who has retired into his workshop to manufacture gold fishes for the rest of his life, is amused by his sons' antics, and before they leave he presents each with a gold fish. On Ash Wednesday, the priest performs the usual anointing of ashes on their forehead—only, on the sons of Aureliano Buendía, they cannot be scrubbed off.

One of the sons, Aureliano Triste, stays in Macondo when his brothers leave. He sets up the ice factory that his predecessor, José Arcadio Buendía, once dreamed of, long ago. In search of a house, he comes upon a seemingly deserted mansion, where he finds Rebeca, still buried in solitude since the death of José Arcadio. She orders him away with a pistol. Úrsula weeps when she hears about Rebeca—not because she realizes that Rebeca is alive, but because she realizes she had forgotten Rebeca entirely. Amaranta, Rebeca's adopted sister, is the only one who remembers, for nothing nourishes memory better than hatred. When Aureliano Triste's sixteen brothers return, a remorseful Úrsula orders Rebeca's broken mansion refurbished at her expense. But the mistress of the house never shows her face. Meanwhile, another of the sons, Aureliano Centeno, opts to join his brother, and, helping with the ice factory management, invents a way to turn fruit juice into ice. Aureliano Triste founds Macondo's first railroad.

Overnight, Macondo becomes an international city. In **chapter 12**, Mr. Herbert, an American, settles in Macondo with partner Mr. Brown and establishes a business selling bananas. Herbert and Brown are decadent, dandified types who surround their houses with electrified chicken wire and collect butterflies. In the meantime, Remedios the Beauty grows more lethally lovely by the day. A man tumbles to his death when he sees her washing herself. Every day she descends to the dining room, there is a disturbance; Úrsula forbids the seventeen Aurelianos to remain in the house. At heart, Remedios remains simple, eating and washing whenever she desires, dining with her hands, and living in the unaffected solitude that men like the Colonel have been striving for most of their lives. While hanging up laundry, Remedios the Beauty is carried up to the sky, the sheets flapping about her. Paradise is the only place where she belongs.

The banana company has brought change. Macondo's new leaders surround themselves with electrified fences, and the streets are patrolled by brutes with machetes who hack grandfathers and little boys to bits. The waste that the company creates is enough to anger Colonel Aureliano Buendía out of his isolation; he vows to Macondo's public to rid the town of those "shitty gringos." That night his sons are assassinated, with boiling lard, rifles, and ice picks; they are easily identified from the crosses of ashes on the foreheads. The feeling in the village is despair—and with good reason, for the banana company will be its downfall. Just as with the real Macondo of García Márquez's childhood, this village, which has struggled through war and disease, will not survive a fruit corporation. Aureliano Buendía tries to enlist the help of his aging friend, Colonel Gerineldo Márquez, to repel the banana company intruders. Márquez—half-paralyzed, jilted by Amaranta, and humiliated by his status as a retired, unneeded fighter—replies, "I already knew that you were old, but now I realize that you're a lot older than you look."

By **chapter 13**, Úrsula is well over one hundred years old and nearing the end of her life. She spends much of these final years in lament—mourning over the confused passage of time; over past mistakes; over loved ones, like Rebeca, whom she has forgotten. She goes blind, but hides it by memorizing the habits of the household and the placements of things. (When Fernanda loses her wedding ring, it is Úrsula who locates it.) The family she has created seems to her ill-starred. With that in mind, she attempts to dissuade Aureliano Segundo from naming his son José Arcadio. Experience has taught her to be wary of the Buendía practice of repetitive naming; a child's fate is decided before the child has had time to live.

Úrsula agrees to the naming only on the condition that she be given exclusive custody of the child. It is on this new José Arcadio that her waning hopes depend. She wants him to become Pope and joins with Fernanda to raise him accordingly. She sends him to a seminary in Rome with bottles of perfumed water and a beribboned hat on his head.

José Arcadio's sister Renata Remedios is a healthy, pleasing adolescent. She practices regularly on her clavichord, enjoys ice cream and new dance steps, and brings her sixty-eight school friends to the Buendía house for a holiday. Her father, Aureliano Segundo, dotes on her. Almost everyone calls her "Meme"—appropriate, as the name resembles neither her mother's nor that of any other Buendía.

With her children away, Fernanda stalks the house in near-mourning, the grim "widow" of a husband who is still alive. Aureliano Segundo has kept up the pretext of waking up with his wife every morning, but now he spends an entire night with Petra Cotes and does not come back. Petra and Aureliano Segundo's passion is at a fury; they caper in a canopied bed with rock crystal mirrors on the ceiling, throw drunken parties, and consume champagne and brandy while their animals copulate with abandon. Aureliano Segundo becomes "fat, purple-colored, turtle-shaped," and enjoys national renown for his insatiable *gourmandise*.

Everyone in the Buendía family continues to revolve, making and unmaking and never moving forward. Petra Cotes and Aureliano Segundo's animals continue to reproduce at the same rate they are slaughtered. Amaranta, who has a visit from Death, weaves her own shroud by day and unravels it at night. Nonetheless, they still entertain the illusion that each day is different—that is, everyone with the exception of Colonel Aureliano Buendía. Aureliano has stopped selling his fishes; those that he forges, he melts down to re-forge the next morning. He has become so senile, so solitary, that he neglects the meals that are brought to him when he is working, forgets what day of the week it is, and speaks not a word. With his eternal smelting, he finds himself in the same loop that trapped his father. On one rainy October day, Colonel Aureliano Buendía sets aside his second fish of the day to go outside to urinate. The circus has come to town, and he ignores it. For the first time since he faced the firing squad, he allows himself to relive the memory of his father taking him to see ice. And when the circus is gone the next morning, his family finds his corpse, attracting vultures underneath the chestnut tree.

Meme blossoms into mischievous womanhood. **Chapter 14** finds her keeping company with the daughters of the American banana merchants, with whom she gets drunk on cane liquor and compares body measurements. Aureliano Segundo takes her to the movies, buys her an English encyclopedia when she expresses the desire to learn the language, and acts as her confidant on the subject of boys. Eager to play the dutiful father now that his daughter is back, he has returned to the Buendía house and to his wife's bed—long enough, anyway, for Fernanda to conceive a daughter, Amaranta Úrsula.

Her namesake, Amaranta, is still haunted by Rebeca. "At times it pained her to have let that outpouring of misery follow its course…but what pained her most and enraged her most and made her most bitter was the fragrant and wormy guava grove of her love that was dragging her toward death." For years Amaranta has planned her adopted sister's death, weaving Rebeca's funeral clothes and planning the perfect last rites. But Amaranta is fated to die first. Luckily she is saved from a resentful ending. Death announces itself to Amaranta several years in advance in the form of a "woman dressed in blue with long hair, with a sort of antiquated look," who instructs the spinster to start sewing her shroud. At first Amaranta buys as much time as she can, through nightly Penelope-like unravelings. But as the years pass, her hatred, as well as her dread of predeceasing her rival, drop away. She calculates the date and hour of her shroud's completion and invites the villagers to give her letters to deliver to the dead when she goes. And so she passes away on the night of February 4, with a box of letters, her last rites performed, her black bandage and virginity intact, and, most importantly, free of the gall that has dominated her life.

While in mourning for her great-aunt, Meme falls in love. Mauricio Babilonia is a mechanic for the banana mogul Mr. Brown and is surrounded by clouds of yellow butterflies wherever he goes. Their affair is abetted by the local champion of love, Pilar Ternera. Eventually, Fernanda catches Meme kissing Mauricio in the movie theatre and imposes a lockdown. The lovers meet secretly every night during Meme's bath, Mauricio's presence causing an invasion of yellow butterflies that Fernanda attempts to kill with insecticide. The affair comes to an abrupt end when Fernanda finds her daughter in her bath surrounded by the mustard plasters used for birth control. The next night Fernanda has a guard shoot Mauricio in the spine—she claims that he is a chicken thief—rendering him an invalid for the rest of his life.

SECTION IV: Chapters 15–20

"The events," **chapter 15** begins, "that would deal Macondo its fatal blow were just showing themselves when they brought Meme Buendía's son home." With this, García Márquez leaps into the final segment of Macondo history. He tells the future—Macondo's fall—and also introduces us to the last Aureliano, "Meme Buendía's son." Every section begins with an Aureliano.

As soon as Fernanda discovers Meme's affair, she orders her on a trip—Meme, who has not spoken a word since her lover was felled by a bullet. Fernanda travels with her across the swamps and leaves her locked in a convent. Fernanda comes back hoping to forget her daughter, only to be followed by a nun bearing Meme's baby in a basket. Fernanda tells everyone that the baby is a foundling from the river.

José Arcadio Segundo, former layabout, has found his calling as a labor organizer. With a commitment echoing that of Colonel Aureliano Buendía, he exposes poor pay and atrocious medical conditions. Mr. Brown and his American compatriots flee. A strike erupts, and the bananas rot because there is no one to pick them. José Arcadio Segundo is at the train station when soldiers fire upon a crowd of strikers—women, men, and children. José Arcadio Segundo collapses, and when he regains consciousness, he is in a train packed with three thousand corpses—"man corpses, woman corpses, child corpses who would be thrown into the sea like rejected bananas." With a "torrential cloudburst," a steady rain begins to fall. When José Arcadio Segundo, who manages to jump off the train, staggers back to Macondo, there is no sign of the massacre in the town streets, and no one recalls having seen any bodies. It is as though the massacre did not take place.

Thus as Macondo careens to its eventual end, so does its memory. In the end, Meme will die, forgotten by those who love her and silent to the end, with her head shaved, in Cracow. Her lover, Mauricio Babilonia, fades from memory; he spends the rest of his life as a bedridden invalid, wrongfully accused of stealing chickens. Their child-to-be is actually born of forgetting, unaware both of his parentage and of the circumstances of his birth. The Buendías forget that they have their patriarch tied to a chestnut tree. Úrsula forgets about her daughter Rebeca, trapped in her moldering house. Amaranta performs perhaps the most significant act of forgetting, for in death she renounces the hatred that kept the past fresh, that became the central narrative of her life. And Úrsula, the one woman who not only remembers but tries to uphold memory (the family pig-tail curse, the eternally lit lamp for the first Remedios), is fading away.

And the speed with which Macondo forgets continues to increase. When banana boss Mr. Brown is brought back to the local court for trial, speaking Spanish and with a Spanish name, no one remembers him, either. The houses occupied by the American banana merchants are torn down. There *was* no banana company. There was no massacre. In Macondo, everyone forgets, but this is the ultimate price of forgetting. If one can forget the little things, one can also forget the slaughter of three thousand. José Arcadio Segundo retires to the old study, where his brother once hid, to devote himself to the perusal of the gypsy's manuscripts. The only person who interrupts him is his mother, Santa Sofía de la Piedad, who leaves his meals on the windowsill; to the rest of the family, he no longer exists.

Chapter 16 opens in a flood. The rain that started falling the night of the massacre will pummel the town for four years, eleven months, and two days. Aureliano Segundo, who has moved back with Petra Cotes since Fernanda took his daughter Meme away, stops by at the Buendía house for a minor business matter and is stranded. People's skin is covered paved with leeches; they need to dig canals to drain water from their houses; their clothing rots into pulp. Around this time, the little Aureliano reveals himself. Despite Fernanda's claims that he is a foundling, he is unmistakably a Buendía, bearing the same brooding stamp of those forbears with whom he shares a name.

Poor Colonel Márquez—scorned by Amaranta, the love of his life, and left alone by the death of the Colonel, his only friend—passes away and is buried in the rain with sodden pomp. When Aureliano Segundo finally summons the energy to check on his mistress, he finds Petra clearing her courtyard of the livestock carcasses. Aureliano Segundo stays for two months, only because it takes him that amount of time to put an oilcloth over his head and head out. The rain has drained everyone's capacity for decision—Úrsula in particular. In her words, "I am only waiting for the rain to stop in order to die." In time, the entire village finds itself waiting for death. Only Gerineldo Márquez will actually die during the storm, though; like Úrsula, no one seems to have the willpower:

> ... sitting in their parlors with an absorbed look and folded arms, feeling unbroken time pass, relentless time,

because it was useless to divide it into months and years, and the days into hours.

The rain can have many meanings but certainly seems retribution for the three thousand forgotten dead. The ceaseless downpour only extends the forgetting. Just as in that long-ago time when the village was infected with insomnia, Macondo's future is on hold.

But the insomnia plague was more playful. Macondo was younger, more innocent, and residents seemed not to mind that they could not remember anything; they were like children. Now that Macondo is more mature, forgetting is less forgivable. The amnesia brought on by the rain is a grim one, and Macondo's inhabitants are all aware, however vaguely, that they are accountable. They are also aware that they are unable to move forward. It was this, the inability to distinguish one day from the next, that drove old José Arcadio Buendía insane.

Úrsula takes refuge in a past that is disordered and vague. She weeps over the death of her great-grandmother, converses with her ancestors, and talks to little Aureliano as if he were her son the Colonel. She is the favorite plaything of the children, who carry her and dress her; she is their babbling, broken-down doll. In fact the only person who does not succumb to the rain is Fernanda. Perhaps it is because she hails from the highlands, where rain is the natural climate; in any case, it intensifies her personality where it has sapped those of the others. Fernanda excoriates her husband with an endless ranting sing-song, an "implacable horse-fly buzzing"—she complains that Macondo is a frying pan of hell, that her husband is a no-good adulterer who keeps an unclean whore. Ultimately it is her ceaseless angry carping that saves the rest of the Buendías from slipping into a near-death lethargy.

Aureliano Segundo is the first to snap from her nagging. He smashes all the valuables in the house, beginning with the begonias and moving onto the Bohemian crystal. Then he stocks the dwindling larder with food. Finally, still humming with energy and irritation, he searches for the coin-filled plaster saint they once disinterred and that Úrsula later hid.

The catatonia brought on by rain is replaced by classic Buendía obsessiveness. Aureliano Segundo wanders about covered with mud, mumbling and eating at odd hours. Physically, he starts looking like an Aureliano, having lost the weight he put during his decadent years with Petra Cotes. He also starts looking once again like his brother José Arcadio Segundo, even though what drives Aureliano is the same hunger for profit that has driven him throughout his adult life. Eventually Aureliano Segundo digs so much into the foundations that the house starts to buckle under itself so seriously that the family thinks it's an earthquake. Then, one Friday afternoon, the sky is lit up by a "crazy crimson sun," and there is no more rain in Macondo for ten years.

The town is a shambles. The streets are swamps, the houses and factories built in the banana fever washed away as if they had never been there. Aureliano Segundo comes home to Petra Cotes to find her thin, weary, full of wrath, but tough as ever. But their ever-reviving wealth has finally been consumed. Petra has fed the house's velvet curtains, Persian carpets, and gold and silver tasseled canopies to her only surviving companion, a mule.

Úrsula's senses return as soon as the rain stops, as does her determination to die—but she realizes that she cannot die before she has brought back her house from the disorder brought on by the years of flood. In **chapter 17** she is once again fighting the encroachments of nature, fighting entropy; in a cleaning frenzy, she drives out the cockroaches, airs out the damp clothes, and clears the rooms of rubble. Finally she opens Melquíades' study and stumbles upon José Arcadio Segundo, who has been hiding during the storm, covered in hair, teeth streaked with slime, and smelling of moss—looking not unlike Melquíades when Melquíades wrote the manuscripts that José Arcadio Segundo now studies. No matter how hard Úrsula tries to persuade him, he will not leave the room.

Aureliano Segundo, now firmly reestablished with Petra Cotes, discovers an entirely different love. Once so profitable, the couple's raffles now earn barely enough to keep them alive.

But they are happier, even though they eat crumbs when they once feasted on whole pigs and champagne. They hold hands, chat into the night, and divide their few coins to buy gifts for those they love. The one to whom they allocate the most money is Fernanda, who in their hearts has become the child they never had. Poverty and compassion suit them better than wealth. Their relationship was once founded on selfishness—money and no children, what García Márquez calls a "sterile complicity." Now, as the self-appointed parents of Fernanda and the Buendía family, they are so happy that even as "two old worn-out people they kept on blooming like little children and playing together like dogs."

As death approaches for Úrsula, so does the increasing realization that "time was not passing...[but] was turning in a circle." Scenes from the past replay. When she spots little Aureliano on the porch, she confuses him with her own son the Colonel. "And now," she tells him, "it's time for you to start learning how to be a silversmith." When she uncovers José Arcadio Segundo in Melquíades' study, she finds herself trapped in the same dialogue that she had with her son the Colonel on the eve of his execution. "What did you expect?" he says, "Time passes."—to which she replies, "That's how it goes, but not so much." Unlike her husband, however, she refuses to find defeat in the absence of victory. She is determined to pass her last days with the same clarity that has characterized her long life. In personality, Úrsula is the blueprint for the Buendía women—they are driven by the very rational concerns of childbirth, jealousy, house renovation, and death. Buendía women are characterized by a lack of imagination, and because of it, they never go insane like their men. Úrsula, however, departs from the world in her own loop, a physical one. Death shrinks her to the size of an infant, and she is buried in a coffin no larger than the basket in which they first received little Aureliano.

The sun burns so hot that birds commit suicide against the windows and the corpse of a man with chopped-off wings cascades from the sky. Rebeca dies in her self-imposed prison at the end of the year, and the village priest, Father Antonio

Isabel, is found playing blind-man's bluff with the village children and dragged to an asylum.

Amaranta Úrsula is sent to private school, and her father, Aureliano Segundo, promises to send her to Brussels to finish her studies. Fernanda, meanwhile, forbids little Aureliano to leave the house, so the villagers will never know that the Buendías are keeping a bastard. As a young girl, Amaranta Úrsula inherits the charms of the Buendía women but without the fatality; she has a hint of the grace of Remedios the Beauty, and the steadfastness of the first Amaranta, but in her slight figure and her energy, she is most like Úrsula. Aureliano is a watery, frail child, eventually educated in Melquíades' workshop by his uncle José Arcadio Segundo.

One morning, Aureliano Segundo wakes up with a knot in his throat. The pains intensify—as if crabs were clawing at his larynx—and he realizes that he is about to die. The only thing that panics him is the fact that he has not yet raised the money to send his daughter to Brussels. He organizes a special raffle of the lands destroyed by the flood, the first raffle that he and Petra Cotes have organized in years that is a spectacular success. Two months later his daughter departs, equipped with the balance of the Buendía riches. Before she reaches Europe, her father dies alone in Fernanda's bedroom, fulfilling his promise to die in her bed. José Arcadio expires at the exact same moment in the workshop, over Melquíades' manuscripts. Knowing of his horror of being buried alive, Santa Sofía de la Piedad cuts José Arcadio Segundo's throat. Aureliano Segundo's former carousing companions contribute a wreath with one of his sayings from his dissipated days: "Cease, cows, for life is short," In the end, Aureliano Segundo's drunken friends bury the twins in the wrong coffins. Despite having grown into very different adults, the twins die as they began— identical, synchronized, and scrambled for the rest of eternity.

One cannot fault Úrsula for mistaking the youngest Aureliano for her own son the Colonel, for the youngest Aureliano grows up to be his mirror image—silent, with an almost pitiless look. He also has inherited something of the first José Arcadio Buendía. **Chapter 18** finds him in the

Buendía library, educating himself on the medieval texts, and tales of exploration and scientific discovery. Next, Aureliano tackles the manuscripts of Melquíades, and this time the gypsy's ghost is on hand to guide him. The manuscripts are finally approaching their one hundredth year, the age at which they are meant to be read.

The house is invaded by red ants and spiders, and this time Santa Sofía de la Piedad, who has run errands and cleaned the house tirelessly for years, cannot get rid of them. Santa Sofía de la Piedad is another victim of the Buendía family's forgetfulness; despite her faithful service, no one remembers that she was wife to the tyrant Arcadio and is the mother of the Segundo twins and Remedios the Beauty. Fernanda, her own daughter-in-law, thinks she is a servant. Frustrated with her battles over the insect infestation—and, presumably, for unknown other reasons—Santa Sofía de la Piedad simply leaves; no one in Macondo notices her departure. The Buendía household now consists of only Aureliano Babilonia and his grandmother Fernanda. They are nourished on weekly baskets of food sent anonymously by Petra Cotes.

Fernanda dies swathed in her moth-eaten queen-of-Madagascar robes, and in death she is more beautiful than ever. Fernanda, who in life asserted that her parents had the God-granted privilege of "remaining intact in their graves with their skin smooth," herself lies unchanged for four months, waiting for her son José Arcadio to return home from Rome to bury her.

As a child, José Arcadio was an asthmatic, insomniac invalid. He grew up in terror. Úrsula used to point to the many saints in the house and tell him that they would inform on him if he did anything bad. Like Aureliano José he had an obsession with his aunt Amaranta, who raised him as a child, powdered him between his legs, and corresponded with him when he was in Rome. As an adult, José Arcadio is a dandy who wears taffeta shirts and takes perfumed baths for two hours; he dropped out of the seminary as soon as he got to Rome, and he has a penchant for playing games with children. Despite his potentially perverse leanings, García Márquez writes, "It was

70

impossible to conceive of a man more like his mother." For while Fernanda was petted and sheltered for her future role as queen, so he was manicured and polished for his expected role as Pope.

The Buendía mansion is transformed into a sinful palace, with crystal mirrors and velvet canopies, where José Arcadio frolics naked with local children in a swimming pool filled with champagne. The children discover the coin-filled plaster saint that Úrsula kept hidden. They also discover Melquíades' manuscript; they try to destroy it, but the manuscript levitates and eludes them until Aureliano returns to rescue it. One night the children wreck José Arcadio's bedroom, and he drives them out with a whip. Not long after, they come back and drown him in his pool. Several hours pass before Aureliano discovers his uncle's bloated corpse, floating in perfumed waters.

By **chapter 19**, the Buendía mansion, with Aureliano Babilonia as its sole occupant, has fallen back into disrepair. Amaranta Úrsula arrives from Brussels with a husband called only Gaston, half a hundred canaries, and endless hatboxes and suitcases. As she looks at the ruins around her, one similarity to old Úrsula becomes clear: "[I]t's obvious that there's no woman in this house!"

She is pretty, provocative, small, indomitable. She makes her husband wear a silk leash around his neck so he will never be unfaithful, as her father was. She scrubs the house and restores it to the gayness it had when Úrsula first installed the pianola, almost a century before. She also does away with the debris of funerals and superstition, for Amaranta Úrsula is a modern girl; the one thing she keeps intact is the altar to her ancestress Remedios Moscote—not from solemnity, but because the idea of having a nine-year-old great-great-grandmother amuses her Amaranta Úrsula dresses fashionably, imports food from Europe, hosts soirées with her old girlfriends on the veranda, and wildly makes love with Gaston on rocking chairs and the parlor floor. Her freshness infects the house, and also its inhabitants. Aureliano starts leaving the house—teaching himself English, French, and Greek on top of the Sanskrit that Melquíades has told him to learn—and frequents the local bookstore, run by a wise man from Catalonia. In that bookstore he makes his first friends. His first sexual encounter is with Nigromanta, a large black woman who sells chicken heads, who teaches him "how to do it like earthworms, then like snails, and finally like crabs."

The only restless person is Gaston. He agreed to come to Macondo for several years, and he loved it at first, eating native food like iguana eggs, and learning how to speak Spanish like a native. But the years have passed, and his young wife shows no sign of wanting to leave. So he reestablishes contact with his old partners in Brussels, dreams of opening an airmail service, and spends much of his time wandering the streets, looking at the sky.

The presence of Amaranta Úrsula causes stirrings in Aureliano—Amaranta Úrsula, the girl with whom he capered as a child and whom he regards as a child. Stirrings turn to obsession, for Aureliano is possessed of the Buendía sexual proclivities; he begs Nigromanta to moan "Gaston" in his ear and weeps at night over Amaranta Úrsula's underwear. He tries to find comfort in the numerous brothels about town. One is a brothel of the imagination, where the invented whores take off their invented dresses, groan, and eat their invented cheese sandwiches. Another is a zoological brothel, where mulatto girls wait upon alligators fat as pigs, white dogs, and snakes with twelve rattles. Finally, Aureliano confesses his love. But Amaranta rejects him, and Aureliano flees to the animal brothel, and the nurturing arms of its proprietress—none other than his great-great-grandmother Pilar Ternera, now one hundred twenty years old. When Aureliano confesses his illicit feelings, she laughs, for "there was no mystery in the heart of a Buendía.... [A] century of cards and experience had taught her that the history of the family was a machine with unavoidable repetitions." "Don't you worry," she assures the boy, "wherever she is right now, she's waiting for you."

Throughout the book, Pilar Ternera has stood on the sensual sidelines—offering her own body or other bodies for frustrated Buendía boys, and generally fanning love's flame. She can be said to be in charge of the reproductive aspect of

Macondo's destiny; she has nurtured many generations of Buendías with both her womb and her influence. But just as she is guardian of its procreation, so is she an instrument of its destruction. She is responsible for keeping Meme and Mauricio's love alive long enough for Aureliano Babilonia—the child who will deal Macondo its "fatal blow"—to be conceived. And in giving Aureliano Babilonia the reassurance he needs to unite with Amaranta Úrsula, she brings about Macondo's final union. Following Pilar Ternera's advice, Aureliano corners Amaranta Úrsula when she is getting out of her bath and her husband is in the next room. There is a struggle, and then they are lovers, culminating in "cat howls" that Amaranta Úrsula has to muffle with a towel for fear of being heard.

Pilar Ternera dies one night in her rocking chair. "It was the end," **chapter 20** intones. Melquíades may be the most powerful fortune teller, but he is an outsider. Pilar Ternera is the fortune teller to whose fate Macondo is linked. It is only fitting that her death should mark the moment when Macondo ceases to have anything left to tell, or, for that matter, anything left to remember. Ternera is the remaining vessel of Macondo's memory. Quietly, the outsiders who have settled in this town leave—first the Catalonian bookshop owner, then Aureliano's foreign friends, and finally Amaranta Úrsula's husband, Gaston, who returns to Brussels. Amaranta Úrsula stops closing up the anthills with quicklime, and they close the doors to the insect infestation and wander around the house naked. The two of them are alone but together, and even more ecstatic when Amaranta Úrsula becomes pregnant. They make no money from the necklaces that Amaranta Úrsula fashions, and yet they survive.

Almost every event in *One Hundred Years of Solitude* echoes at least one other. Petra Cotes becomes the mistress of two brothers, just as Pilar Ternera before her; a massacre of banana tree workers mirrors the earlier massacre of festival workers; and Colonel Aureliano Buendía—the most mysterious character of the book, and arguably the central character—is plagued by a war that is an endless return; when he finally pulls out of it, he walks back to the workshop to hammer gold fishes as before. At no points, however, does the mirroring seem more deliberate than in the first five chapters and the last five. Macondo is deliberately unraveled as it was woven, just as Amaranta once unwove her shroud and the Colonel melted down his fishes. Hence, Aureliano is the original Aureliano and also the original José Arcadio, Amaranta Úrsula is Úrsula and also every other female in the book—with Remedios' beauty, Rebeca's ability to love, and the original Amaranta's penchant for sewing and also for attracting nephews. Under the last José Arcadio, the house is restored to the decadence it enjoyed in Aureliano Segundo's time; then it falls into same disrepair it saw during the war; Amaranta Úrsula restores it to the purer glory it enjoyed when Úrsula first had the pianola installed. Like Rebeca, Amaranta Úrsula is pledged to one man but leaves him for a boy she considers to be her brother. Gaston pursues his airmail idea with the same assiduity with which the first José Arcadio tried to link Macondo to the outside world. Due to the encroachment of the ants, Amaranta Úrsula and Aureliano are restricted to quarters that are roughly the size of the original house before Úrsula expanded it. Outsiders depart in the reverse of the order in which they arrived: first the banana company, then the foreign settlers, then Melquíades, and ultimately Pilar Ternera.

The only significant difference is in the first and last José Arcadios. They are the only characters to actually share exactly the same name—all other names are variations—and patriarch and pedophile are farcical opposites. The first José Arcadio dreamed of worlds abroad and never reached them, and the last went abroad and accomplished nothing. The first José Arcadio babbled Latin like a first language; the last José Arcadio was supposed to have learned it but never did. The first spends his final days tied to a tree, forgotten, and the last floats in a pool, unfound.

Amaranta Úrsula is determined to name her son Rodrigo, to break the Buendía cycle, but Aureliano insists on naming the child Aureliano. True to Úrsula's ancient fears, the boy has the tail of a pig. Tellingly, neither parent knows of the curse; with

Pilar Ternera's death, there is no one left who remembers. Soon after the birth, Amaranta Úrsula begins bleeding uncontrollably, and she dies. Crushed with grief, Aureliano abandons the baby, repairing to a bar and eventually to the attentions of Nigromanta, who cleans him of his tears and vomit. When he finally stumbles back to the Buendía house the baby is missing; when he finds it, it is being eaten by the ants. Suddenly we abandon the echoes and enter into a series of firsts: Amaranta Úrsula is the first Buendía woman to die in childbirth; Aureliano is the first Buendía man to *flee* solitude in his misery, rather than to search for it. The infant Aureliano may not be the first baby with a pig's tail, but he is the first to die in infancy. At the end of these firsts, another—Melquíades' manuscript is ready to be read, after a hundred years, and Aureliano Babilonia will be the one to read it.

It is a history of Macondo. There are three layers of deciphering: first the Sanskrit in which it is written, then the archaic codes found in the wise Catalonian's bookshop. The third layer of code breaks by itself: a code of time. Melquíades' parchments, like the novel, is not linear, but cyclic; the one hundred years are encapsulated at once, and as befits a city that is born backwards, the end precedes the beginning. Appropriately, the first line that Aureliano translates is the last one: "The first is to be tied to a tree and the last is being eaten by ants." Aureliano reads about the birth of Remedios the Beauty, the most beautiful woman in the world. He reads about his conception in a bathtub surrounded by mustard plasters and yellow butterflies. He reads that he is his lover's nephew. Finally, Aureliano reads his own fate, and knows that he is never to leave this room. Macondo is destined to be ripped away by the winds, and to take Aureliano with it.

It has been argued that Aureliano is doomed by his last name, for he is technically Aureliano Babilonia, after his father, which marks him as Babylon's son. But there are other, more potent reasons. An officer after the ill-fated banana strike summarizes Macondo's hundred years: "Nothing has happened in Macondo, nothing has ever happened, and nothing ever will happen." Out of a relationship built on echoes—incest between aunt and nephew, a son with a pig's tail, and the duplicated qualities of their personalities—Aureliano and Amaranta Úrsula have created change. And once something happens, once something *changes*, Macondo collapses.

Most important, Aureliano and Amaranta Úrsula are doomed because, as Michael Wood points out, they are happy. More to the point, they are happy *together*. "The cards," Wood writes, "are stacked against...any love which might lead [a couple] out of solitude." (Wood, 86) Every Buendía—every character of importance—dies alone, whether it is José Arcadio Buendía under the chestnut tree or Pilar Ternera in her rocking chair. Even the couples who have approached conjugal happiness—Petra Cotes and Aureliano Segundo, José Arcadio and Rebeca—die by themselves. Amaranta Úrsula, on the other hand, is the first Buendía to die with the man she loves by her bedside.

Solitude for García Márquez is not to be avoided, but exalted. This is an attitude that is not only cultivated by the author, but by the society which reared him; García Márquez's own sister is called Soledad. (Bell, 68) Solitude for García Márquez is a kind of lost mythic paradise, and with few exceptions all the characters spend their lives pursuing it. But solitude and happiness are not compatible; solitude is melancholy, born of suffering and introspection. Amaranta Úrsula and Aureliano reject solitude's paradise for the pleasures they share. Aureliano Babilonia greets solitude with mourning. In being modern and lovingly self-serving, Amaranta Úrsula and Aureliano are unknowing sinners. When Amaranta Úrsula throws out the family relics, she also trashes the family commitment to loneliness, and thus to God. Macondo evaporates in paradox; its repeated history has become "unrepeatable," its repetitive people losing their "second opportunity."

As tenderly constructed as the Buendías are, they leave us uneasy. For keeping them together is ultimately fear—of progress and of love. Even Úrsula, when given the chance, would prefer to return rather than to move forward. On her watch, the Buendía mansion is restored, rather than rebuilt; in its various "happy" periods, it is exactly as it has been before. Buendías have a zealous commitment to feeding a cycle that ultimately absolves each of them, but also leaves them isolated. The sanctimonious Fernanda may suit them more than they would like to admit, for she ensures the solitude of everyone she loves—forcing her husband to die alone in his bed, and trapping her daughter behind convent doors.

There is very little joy in the Buendía family; every time joy approaches, some massive tragedy is always there to check it. Images abound, antiquated and claustrophobic—a gaunt Colonel who forges fishes, an imprisoned beauty with no thought for men, an asthmatic little boy terrified of the life-size saints that glower at him in the night. They live in marked contrast to the cheerful characters that populate the last section of the novel. García Márquez borrowed from the ones he loved as a boy to be the core of *One Hundred Years of Solitude*; but in its last pages, he borrows those people he loved as a man. Alfonso, Germán, Alvaro, and indeed Gabriel—the coterie that congregates at the Catalonian's bookstore—are actually García Márquez's friends from his days in Barranquilla. They are a jolly, noisy flock, preoccupied with the modern world of New York and Paris and girlfriends. Merely passers-by, they can enjoy life without consequences. Poor Aureliano José is not so lucky. He is bound to the Buendías, and in finding joy he has betrayed them. Can we really, therefore, endorse a universe in which a bile-filled Amaranta has a place, but where cheerful, curious, and sometimes tempestuous characters like Aureliano José and Amaranta Úrsula are considered sinners, merely because they are successful in love? Perhaps this is what García Márquez meant when he said in his Nobel Prize acceptance speech that he hoped for "A new and sweeping utopia of life, where no one will be able to decide for others how they die, where love will prove true, and happiness be possible, and where the races condemned to one hundred years of solitude will have, at last and forever, a second opportunity on earth." Though he clearly adores the superstitious, ghostly roots of his forebears, García Márquez may be telling us that it is time for Colombia to move on. His vision in *One Hundred Years* is pessimistic, but his hopes for his own world are far from it.

Bibliography

Bell, Michael. *Gabriel García Márquez: Solitude and Solidarity*. Modern Novelists series. St. Martin's Press, 1993.

García Márquez, Gabriel. *Living to Tell the Tale*. Alfred A. Knopf, 2003.

———. *One Hundred Years of Solitude*. Perennial Classics, 1998.

McNerney, Kathleen. *Understanding Gabriel García Márquez*. University of South Carolina Press, 1989.

Ortega, Julio, ed. *Gabriel García Márquez and the Powers of Fiction*. Texas Pan American series. University of Texas Press, 1988.

Wood, Michael. *Gabriel García Márquez: One Hundred Years of Solitude*. Landmarks of World Literature series. Cambridge University Press, 1990.

LORRAINE ELENA ROSES ON IMAGES OF WOMEN IN THE NOVEL

First, I propose that the dichotomy between the "good" and the "bad" women should be dismantled and reconfigured as a dialectic and a progression in which the socially elite women struggle to wield social power over the transgressive or abject members of their sex, while simultaneously being challenged and influenced by them. For instance, Úrsula's superior social position as the wife of the patriarch contrasts with the subaltern position of Pilar Ternera, a free agent active in the transgressive sphere of sex work. These characters at the subaltern end of the continuum move in and out of the Buendía household. By sharing physical space and by sustaining sexual bonds with the Buendía men, the marginal women evince qualities repressed by institutionalized propriety and assert a connection to those who paradoxically depend on them. The elite women (such as Úrsula), though they provide stability, strength, and productivity, have been socialized in such a way that they cannot supply the sensuality and eroticism sought by their Buendía consorts. As a result and through these subtle interconnections, both classes of women inhabit a continuum of defining characteristics that mutually reinforce, rather than oppose, each other. A fine example is Pilar, to whom Úrsula's sons turn for sexual initiation and through whom they procreate the next generation of Buendías.

The trajectory of the female characters throughout the novel and the agency exercised by them reveal a pattern of symbiosis. The entrepreneurial and self-sacrificing pillars of the Buendía family are portrayed throughout as sanctimonious and rigid; their puritanical primness, spiritual shortcomings, and pretensions to grandeur are inscribed in the text with deeply ironic negativity. The tendency that begins in Úrsula as an incapacity to accept the marriage of her son to his foster sister gradually morphs into the murderous intolerance of Fernanda, with the resultant maiming of her transgressive daughter's lover, Mauricio Babilonia, and the exile of this daughter to a convent in Cracow. Remedios, la Bella, another socially elite woman, is metonymically connected to death, for the sight of her causes men to lose consciousness or die in the attempt to be with her, such as the young man who climbs onto a shaky roof to view her in the bath; yet a third Buendía woman, Remedios's Aunt Amaranta, drives her refined Italian suitor to suicide.

The hard-working and emotionally vibrant Pilar, by contrast, perpetuates the Buendía lineage, while radiating a compassionate tenderness, an erotic enthusiasm, and a stamina absent in the characters of Úrsula and Fernanda. She endures past the age of 145, still stationed at the door of her sexual "paradise" (García Márquez, 404). The characteristics of Petra Cotes—fertility, eroticism, and clairvoyance—highlight, by the same token, a dimension of female power previously unexplored by literary critiques of *One Hundred Years of Solitude*.

It should be clear that the socially marginal, abject women occupy, *alongside the elites*, a privileged space in the novel. Absent Pilar Ternera and her ilk, the Buendía men would falter in their cognitive and philosophical mission. These women enable the male search for knowledge of their origins, the very intellectual and spiritual quest that drives the narrative. Rather than merely serving as a foil for the legitimate Buendía women—their alleged opposites in the "good/bad" dichotomy—transgressive women hold a powerful position intrinsically related to the principles that govern the novel. Although these women do not directly participate in the intellectual adventure of deciphering Melquíades's manuscript, nor do they receive the tutelage of the semidivine gypsy, they follow the path to knowledge in a transcendent sense, one of mythic and quasi-biblical dimensions. With a sustaining immanent wisdom complementary to that stored in the manuscripts of Melquíades, these female characters, down the generations, illuminate a path toward possible redemption through love.

Pilar Ternera's character embodies the paradigm that illustrates this point. Of all the characters in the novel, only she is present throughout—even the critics who regard her as but a "grotesque replica of Úrsula" (Deveny and Marcos, 86) have noted her pervasive presence during the narrative. She arrives in the Buendía household to "help with the domestic tasks" (García Márquez, 29) and progresses from managing kitchen chores to initiating (on her own terrain) the Buendía sons into manhood and procreation. In that she also has the power to heal and to read the future in the tarot, her knowledge clearly transcends the cult of domesticity. During the family's plague of forgetfulness and insomnia, Pilar inverts her art, "when she conceived the trick of reading the past in the cards as she had read the future before" (García Márquez, 49). Úrsula, Rebeca, and Meme continue to seek out Pilar and her cards, as do the men during times of doubt or crisis. Clearly, Pilar, as the character who possesses the primordial traits of fertility and memory, occupies a primary and critical space in the novel—a position of power that previous critiques have erroneously overlooked or obscured.

Pilar ages alone, yet the loss of her youth only enhances her knowledge and generosity. Described as a "sorceress" and "prophetess," Pilar and her potent spirit call to the Buendías generation after generation, and it is she who gives birth to first offspring of the Buendía men born in Macondo. At the interruption of the repeated cycling of time, Pilar remains the clairvoyant, the counselor, the first in a chain of characters who procreate with and comfort the Buendía males, sustain them, and act to enable the decoding of the revelatory manuscripts. Pilar's fundamental and pivotal functions reveal that her character, far from being incidental, is necessary to the novel. How, then, to read the re-creation of such a role in at least three more women, including Petra Cotes, Santa Sofía de la Piedad, and Nigromanta?

CLIVE GRIFFIN ON HUMOR IN
ONE HUNDRED YEARS OF SOLITUDE

Some theoreticians of humour concentrate on the sort of subjects which are 'inherently comical', maintaining, for example, that one universal source of laughter in Western societies is the violation of taboos. The commonest of these subjects concern sexual or other bodily functions. *One Hundred Years* abounds with such scenes. José Arcadio's Herculean strength and stature may be funny enough in itself, but even more so is his minutely described and 'incredible member, covered with a maze of blue and red tattoos written in several languages' (p. 84),[6] a fitting forebear of Aureliano Babilonia's equally astonishing appendage on which, at the end of the novel, he balances a bottle of beer as he cavorts drunkenly round one of Macondo's brothels. Scenes of sexual intercourse cause us to smile either because of their exuberant eroticism, like the seismic orgasms enjoyed by José Arcadio and Rebeca, or because of some of the female characters' ridiculous prudery: Úrsula is reluctant to remove her chastity belt and consummate her marriage, and Fernanda obeys a calendar of 'prohibited days' on which she refuses to grant the husband whom she later describes as her 'rightful despoiler' even the frigid submission which characterizes their physical relationship. Deviation provides even more fun: José Arcadio Segundo and the local verger have a penchant for she-asses; Amaranta is a maiden aunt who, even when old, is the object of incestuous fantasies for generations of Buendías; not only is the effete Pietro Crespi thought to be a homosexual,[7] but Catarino is known to be one; there is even a dog in the 'zoological brothel' which is described as 'a gentle pederast who, nevertheless, serviced bitches to earn his keep' (p. 333). Similarly, García Márquez employs lavatorial jokes, describing the complexities of entertaining sixty-eight school-girls and four nuns in a house with only one toilet, or the pungency of José Arcadio's flatulence which makes flowers wither on the spot.

Taboos are not limited to bodily functions. Death and religion are a source of jokes in most societies, the latter being even more piquant in as conservatively Catholic a country as Colombia. In *One Hundred Years* most of the characters either fade away in old age (José Arcadio Buendía, the Colonel, Úrsula, Rebeca, and Melquíades) or else their deaths are treated with black humour. José Arcadio's corpse emits such an evil stench that his mourners decide in desperation to 'season it with pepper, cumin and laurel leaves and boil it over a gentle heat for a whole day' (p. 118); the body of Fernanda's distinguished father—appropriately enough a Knight of the Order of the Holy Sepulchre—spent so long on its journey to Macondo that when the coffin was opened 'the skin had erupted in stinking belches and was simmering in a bubbling, frothy stew' (p. 186); a drunken funeral party buries the twins, José Arcadio Segundo and Aureliano Segundo, in each other's graves thus putting the final touch to the running joke about their muddled identities.

Fernanda's stuffy religiosity makes her the butt of numerous comic scenes but, more subtly and with nice irony, the narrator claims that the indelible cross worn by all of the Colonel's campaign sons will guarantee their safety yet, in the end, their murderers recognize them precisely by this sacred sign. A statue of St Joseph revered by Úrsula turns out to be merely a hiding place for the gold which enables a renegade apprentice Pope to indulge in orgies with his potential catamites while obsessed by incestuous desires for his great-great aunt.

The final taboo is a linguistic one, for the dialogue of *One Hundred Years* is a convincing representation of the expression of uncultured characters for whom expletives are part of everyday speech. These are frequently used comically to deflate scenes which are in danger of becoming over-sentimental. For example, the amiable Gerineldo Márquez's grief at being rejected by Amaranta is reflected by a sympathetic Nature; he sends his comrade, the Colonel, a poignant message, 'Aureliano, it is raining in Macondo' only to receive the reply, 'Don't be a prick, Gerineldo. Of course it's raining; it's August' (p. 144).

The violation of these taboos is never prurient. The author treats sex, death, religion and language with a light-hearted candour. Indeed, as Aureliano Segundo observes when he sees Fernanda's prim nightdress which covers her from head to foot but has 'a large, round, delicately trimmed hole over her lower stomach' (p. 182), it is prudishness which is really obscene. Similarly, euphemism leads only to pain and ridicule: Fernanda seeks a cure for her medical condition but, as she cannot bring herself to describe the embarrassing symptoms openly, the invisible doctors are unable to diagnose her complaint and she is condemned to a life of suffering.

Renaissance theorists of comedy, understandably enough, did not identify the contravention of such taboos as a source of humour; rather, they conjectured more abstractly that it was the provocation of wonderment and surprise in the reader or spectator which caused mirth.[8] Such wonderment lies at the heart of much of the laughter of *One Hundred Years* where García Márquez has frequent recourse to exaggeration, fantasy, and the ridiculous. While we are willing to accept that José Arcadio returns from his travels a grown man, the exaggeration with which his exploits and appetites are recounted either leads the reader to reject the novel as nonsense or, as Forster has it, to pay the extra sixpence at the fair and revel in fantasy and hyperbole.[9] Just as he laughs at the reaction of the naive inhabitants of Macondo whose description of the first train to be seen in the town is of 'a terrifying object like a kitchen pulling a village' (p. 192), so the reader is invited to laugh at his own reaction when his expectations of the narrative are challenged and he has to suspend his normal judgement about what is possible in reality and fiction and what is not. It is with wonderment that he learns of a fantastic character like Melquíades who frequently returns from the land of the dead but who grows old there just as people do in the land of the living, of the appearance of the Duke of Marlborough (the 'Mambrú' of the traditional Spanish nursery rhyme) at the Colonel's side in the civil war, or of other equally fantastic situations, often described in absurdly precise detail, such as the love-making of Petra Cotes and Aureliano Segundo which increases the numbers of their livestock overnight. Although the fantasy is often an extension of, or a metaphor for reality, such wonderment provokes laughter. A situation, an event, or a character may start out as entirely credible, but by a logical development *ad absurdum* they become comical. Thus we understand that Fernanda and Úrsula, following a well-established tradition among upper-crust Colombian families, should wish José Arcadio, their only legitimate son and great-great-grandson, to enter the church; their ambition only becomes humorous because they are determined that he should not be just any sort of priest and set about grooming him from childhood for the job of Pope. On other occasions, however, the comedy resides in astonishing us by gratuitous details—José Arcadio Buendía can increase his weight at will—or by a challenge to our notions of cause and effect either through the events of the novel or the illogicality of the characters' reasoning: thus, for instance, Francis Drake comes to Riohacha exclusively to set in motion the events of the novel which will eventually lead to the birth of a baby with a pig's tail; when Melquíades's breath begins to smell, he is given a bath.

Notes

6. All page references are to the Editorial Sudamerica 1975 edition. The Translations are my own.

7. Pietro Crespi is also given a comically inappropriate name: it recalls Pedro Crespo, one of the best-known figures from Spanish drama of the seventeenth century, where he is the major character in Pedro Calderón de la Barca's *El alcalde de Zalamea*; Crespo, far from being an effete Italian, was a forceful and cunning Spanish peasant.

8. Russell, "DonQuixote," p. 321.

9. E.M. Forster, *Aspects of the Novel* (Harmondsworth, 1977), pp. 103–104.

PETER H. STONE AND GABRIEL GARCÍA MÁRQUEZ DISCUSS THE CREATION OF THE NOVEL

GARCÍA MÁRQUEZ: After *In Evil Hour* I did not write anything for five years. I had an idea of what I always wanted to do, but there was something missing and I was not sure what it was until one day I discovered the right tone—the tone that I eventually used in *One Hundred Years of Solitude*. It was based on the way my grandmother used to tell her stories. She told things that sounded supernatural and fantastic, but she told them with complete naturalness. When I finally discovered the tone I had to use, I sat down for eighteen months and worked every day.

INTERVIEWER: How did she express the "fantastic" so naturally?

GARCÍA MÁRQUEZ: What was most important was the expression she had on her face. She did not change her expression at all when telling her stories and everyone was surprised. In previous attempts to write *One Hundred Years of Solitude*, I tried to tell the story without believing in it. I discovered that what I had to do was believe in them myself and write them with the same expression with which my grandmother told them: with a brick face.

INTERVIEWER: There also seems to be a journalistic quality to that technique or tone. You describe seemingly fantastic events in such minute detail that it gives them their own reality. Is this something you have picked up from journalism?

GARCÍA MÁRQUEZ: That's a journalistic trick which you call also apply to literature. For example, if you say that there are elephants flying in the sky, people are not going to believe you. But if you say that there are four hundred and twenty-five elephants in the sky, people will probably believe you. *One Hundred Years of Solitude* is full of that sort of thing. That's exactly the technique my grandmother used. I remember particularly the story about the character who is surrounded by yellow butterflies. When I was very small there was an electrician who came to the house. I became very curious because he carried a belt with which he used to suspend himself from the electrical posts. My grandmother used to say that every time this man came around, he would leave the house full of butterflies. But when I was writing this, I discovered that if I didn't say the butterflies were yellow, people would not believe it. When I was writing the episode of Remedios the Beauty going to heaven it took me a long time to make it credible. One day I went out to the garden and saw a woman who used to come to the house to do the wash and she was putting out the sheets to dry and there was a lot of wind. She was arguing with the wind not to blow the sheets away. I discovered that if I used the sheets for Remedios the Beauty, she would ascend. That's how I did it, to make it credible. The problem for every writer is credibility. Anybody can write anything so long as it's believed.

INTERVIEWER: What was the origin of the insomnia plague in *One Hundred Years of Solitude*?

GARCÍA MÁRQUEZ: Beginning with Oedipus, I've always been interested in plagues. I have studied a lot about medieval plagues. One of my favorite books is *The Journal of the Plague Years* by Daniel Defoe, among other reasons because Defoe is a journalist who sounds like what he is saying is pure fantasy. For many years I thought Defoe had written about the London plague as he observed it. But then I discovered it was a novel, because Defoe was less than seven years old when the plague occurred in London. Plagues have always been one of my recurrent themes—and in different forms. In *In Evil Hour* the pamphlets are plagues. For many years I thought that the political violence in Colombia had the same metaphysics as the plague. Before *One Hundred Years of Solitude*, I had used a plague to kill the birds in a story called "The Day After Saturday." In *One Hundred Years of Solitude* I used the insomnia plague as something of a literary trick since it's the opposite of the sleeping plague. Ultimately, literature is nothing but carpentry.

INTERVIEWER: Can you explain that analogy a little more?

GARCÍA MÁRQUEZ: Both are very hard work. Writing something is almost as hard as making a table. With both you are working with reality, a material just as hard as wood. Both are full of tricks and techniques. Basically very little magic and a lot of hard work are involved. And as Proust, I think, said, it takes ten percent inspiration and ninety percent perspiration. I never have done any carpentry but it's the job I admire most, especially because you can never find anyone to do it for you.

INTERVIEWER: What about the banana fever in *One Hundred Years of Solitude*? How much of that is based on what the United Fruit Company did?

GARCÍA MÁRQUEZ: The banana fever is modeled closely on reality. Of course, I've used literary tricks on things which have not been proved historically. For example, the massacre in the square is completely true but while I wrote it on the basis of testimony and documents, it was never known exactly how many people were killed. I used the figure three thousand, which is obviously an exaggeration. But one of my childhood memories was watching a very, very long train leave the plantation supposedly full of bananas. There could have been three thousand dead on it, eventually to be dumped in the sea. What's really surprising is that now they speak very naturally in the Congress and the newspapers about the "three thousand dead." I suspect that half of all our history is made in this fashion. In *The Autumn of the Patriarch*, the dictator says it doesn't matter if it's true now, because sometime in the future it will be true. Sooner or later people believe writers rather than the government.

INTERVIEWER: That makes the writer pretty powerful, doesn't it?

GARCÍA MÁRQUEZ: Yes, and I can feel it too. It gives me a great sense of responsibility. What I would really like to do is a piece of journalism which is completely true and real, but which sounds as fantastic as *One Hundred Years of Solitude*. The more I live and remember things from the past the more I think that literature and journalism are closely related.

GENE H. BELL-VILLADA ON MÁRQUEZ AND THE YANKEE CHARACTER

García Márquez's own Yankees are pure caricature but are drawn with such virtuoso precision and elaborate complexity that, both in aesthetic effect and in narrative significance, the portraits are fully achieved. The scene in which the Buendías guest Mr. Herbert tastes a banana, opens his toolbox, and then successively applies to the innocent fruit his optical instruments, special scalpel, pharmacist's scale, gunsmith's calipers, and thermometer and photometer is a perfect satire of our notorious mercantile-technological fix, our mania for bringing to bear the latest and most sophisticated hardware onto the simplest of things (213).[7] At some point in his career, García Márquez appears to have understood that too solemn a vision of U.S. imperialism contributes nothing to the art of friction and that on the other hand there exists a rich potential in exaggerating and ridiculing those technological obsessions of ours that, even in the years since his novel was first published, have become baroque and even grotesque.

García Márquez explained to me in an interview that his Yankees are depicted as the Macondoites perceive them—a key aspect of his novel.[8] To us in our time, American global power—with its worldwide extractive and agricultural, manufacturing, marketing, financial, military, and media apparatus—is a fact we routinely take for granted as a given. For early twentieth-century Macondoites, however, the "gringos" are a novelty, and it is thus that García Márquez succeeds in defamiliarizing his Americans, "making strange" their wondrous technology and their "languid wives in muslin dresses and large veiled hats," and the almost fantastical milieu of their town across the tracks, with its "streets lined with palm trees, houses with screened windows, small white tables on the terraces, ... and extensive blue lawns with peacocks and quails" (214).

Such a description suggests Los Angeles in the 1910s (or in the movie *El Norte*'s 1980s). In the context of a tropical and less-developed Macondo, however, the entire ensemble is intrusive, virtually something from another planet. Neither the townspeople nor we readers can hope to penetrate that colonial enclave, save for Meme's consortings with the Browns, and even then all is seen through her tender adolescent eyes. The narrator of *One Hundred Years of Solitude* is of the omniscient kind, as critics often note, but the actual bounds of such omniscience lie precisely in the electrified fence surrounding and protecting the gringos' separate reality.

By so depicting his Americans, García Márquez adhered to the first and basic rule of every good writer—namely "Write about what you know best."

(...)

It's well worth noting that, in all the Banana Company-related episodes in *One Hundred Years of Solitude*, there is but a single occasion in which an American character is directly quoted, and that rare utterance is relayed to us secondhand, via an unreliable source. I am referring to the government's proclamation that, following assurances that the strike had been peacefully settled, cites Mr. Brown as affirming that labor negotiations will resume "When the rain stops. As long as the rain lasts we're suspending all activities" (287).[11] The truth is that the rain will fall for almost a half decade and heap ruin on Macondo.

In his numerous interviews and journalistic writings, García Márquez always demonstrates an excellent knowledge of United States history and culture. Moreover, he lived in New York in 1960 and 1961, and then, en route to Mexico, he traveled through the southern states (where, owing to Jim Crow laws, he and his family experienced some difficulty in finding hotel rooms). And yet he has never presumed to know the more intimately psychological, existential aspect of American life. Nevertheless, the Colombian novelist was to make the most out of his small-town Caribbean point of view, transforming this perspective into a narrative strength and casting the mold for the satirical vision he at last articulates toward that most classic of U.S. agribusiness firms.

Notes

7. All page references will be provided within the body of the text.

8. As García Márquez observed to me, "The Yankees are depicted the way the local people saw them...." See the interview in this volume.

11. In the original, Mr. Brown's alleged comment is in standard, correct Spanish: "Será cuando escampe. Mientras dure la lluvia , suspendemos toda clase de actividades." Gabriel García Márquez, *Cien años de soledad* (Buenos Aires: Editorial Sudamericana, 1969), p. 262.

ANÍBAL GONZÁLEZ ON MÁRQUEZ'S USE OF JOURNALISTIC TECHNIQUES

During his years as a struggling young author, García Márquez worked not merely as a columnist or literary journalist, as Borges, Carpentier, and others had, but also as a reporter. His work in the Colombian newspapers *El Universal*, *El Heraldo*, and *El Espectador*, the Venezuelan magazines *Momento* and *Venezuela Gráfica*, and the Cuban press agency Prensa Latina required him not only to write social chronicles and film reviews, but also to do investigative reporting. In a recent interview with Plinio Apuleyo Mendoza, García Márquez claims that in 1951, when he first heard about the events of which he later wrote in *Chronicle of a Death Foretold*, "they didn't interest me as material for a novel but as a subject for a reportage. But that was a poorly developed genre in Colombia in those days, and I was a provincial journalist in a local newspaper which perhaps would not be interested in the affair." In 1955, he wrote a series of articles about the experiences of a Colombian sailor who spent ten days shipwrecked. Although they were based on García Márquez's interview with the sailor, the articles showed, probably because of their subject matter, a markedly novelistic character.

(...)

In recent interviews, García Márquez has remarked that his journalistic practice did not aid him, "as has been said, to find an efficacious language. Journalism taught me stratagems to give validity to my stories. Giving Remedios the Beautiful sheets (white sheets) in order to make her go up into heaven, or giving a cup of chocolate (and not another drink) to father Nicanor Reina before he levitates ten centimeters above the ground are very useful tricks of journalistic precision." He continues, "the language I used in *No One Writes to the Colonel, In Evil Hour,* and several of the stories in *Big Mama's Funeral* is concise, sober, dominated by a concern for efficacy that comes from journalism." García Márquez also frequently insists on his stories' foundations in empirical reality: "There is not a single line in my novels which is not based on reality." García Márquez sees journalism's influence on his work not so much as a matter of style, but as one of rhetorical stratagems which he uses to give verisimilitude to his stories.

(...)

Journalism is not thematized in García Márquez's undisputed masterpiece, *One Hundred Years of Solitude* (1967), but it is not difficult to see that the saga of Macondo, with its implicit (and occasionally explicit) meditation about the problems of writing and history in Spanish America, could only have been written after the deconstruction of old-fashioned critical ideologies, by an appeal to journalism, in "Big Mama's Funeral." There is also, perhaps, a subtle reminiscence of journalism in *One Hundred Years of Solitude*'s parody of history-writing, particularly in Melquíades' manuscript, which, surpassing journalism, prophesies, in minute—journalistic?—detail, the future history of Macondo.

STEPHEN MINTA ON THE BANANA COMPANY MASSACRE

García Márquez seems to be concerned with three important issues in his reconstruction of the Ciénaga massacre. First, there is his natural sympathy with the position of the strikers, with their demands for better living and working conditions, with the general political dimension of the strike. Second, there is his desire to rescue from a continuing conspiracy of silence an important event in the history of Colombia. The fact that neither of those who witnessed the massacre is able to persuade others of the truth about what happened is a reflection both of the fear which later silenced so many of those who took part in the events of 1928, and of the unwillingness of the Colombian establishment to acknowledge its share of responsibility. This large-scale, collective repression of the past has potentially lethal consequences. For once you fail to admit the existence of something important in your past, you are close to denying the past any significance at all; and, from then on, it is easy to deprive the present and the future of all significance too. In their submission to a process of wilful forgetfulness; the people of Macondo are taking a road that leads towards the picture-postcard cliché of the endlessly backward, yet always happily smiling, group of natives, caught in the illusion of an eternal circularity, reduced to a passivity which only the intrusion of an historical perspective might work to disturb. This process of repression can be seen in the response of the woman whom José Arcadio Segundo meets as he escapes from the train that is carrying away the dead. The woman may well have lost members of her own family in the massacre; she must, at least, have some idea of what has occurred, but she says: 'There haven't been any dead here'; and she adds: 'Since the time of your uncle, the colonel, nothing has happened in Macondo.' That is precisely the attitude which the establishment seeks to create. A little later, as the leaders of the strike are being systematically rounded up by the military and killed, we have a confirmation of the 'official view'. Relatives of the dead and missing come in search of news, but the army officers tell them: 'You must have been dreaming ... Nothing has happened in Macondo, nothing is happening, and nothing will ever happen. This is a happy town.'

García Márquez's third area of interest, in connexion with the Ciénaga massacre, relates to a question that recurs frequently in his writing: what can anyone legitimately seek to know about the 'truth' of an historical event? Something clearly happened in the square in Ciénaga, but what exactly? What is recoverable?

(...)

Lucila Inés Mena and Gustavo Alfaro have gathered together, in their respective books, a fascinating collection of accounts relating to the period, some of which fail to mention the massacre in Ciénaga at all, while others reveal radically differing attitudes in respect of the scale and ultimate importance of what took place, with widely differing casualty statistics to support their various positions. So García Márquez's own account of the massacre, with its conscious exaggerations, is also a reminder that all versions of the past are incurably fictitious; and the reader is thus further prepared for the conclusion of the novel, with its deeply self-dramatizing conviction that literature can never bring the past back to life, and its clear challenge to recognize that what we have been reading has, of course, been a fiction all along.

STEPHEN MINTA ON THE SIGNIFICANCE OF MELQUÍADES'S MANUSCRIPT

The reader has been aware, from very early on in the book, of the existence of Melquíades's manuscripts, but, until the last moment, their precise content and status remain obscure.

Aureliano Segundo attempts to decipher the texts at a point about half way through the novel, but Melquíades tells him, in a visitation, that the manuscripts can only be understood when they have reached one hundred years of age; and this is the clue to the fact that what the parchments contain is Melquíades's account written in advance and with full foreknowledge, of the one hundred years of the Buendía family that are also the subject of the novel we are reading. José Arcadio Segundo, in his turn, attempts a decipherment, and it is he who initiates the young Aureliano in the study of the texts. Aureliano will complete the decipherment, and, at that point, the novel will end. Aureliano shares a privileged relationship with the narrator, and is clearly designated as a source of knowledge within the book. It is he, alone of all the characters, who accepts what José Arcadio Segundo has to say about the massacre of the banana workers. It is he who discovers that the language of Melquíades's manuscripts is Sanskrit, and, in the final moments, it is he who finds the code which renders the texts intelligible.

The point at which everything becomes clear to Aureliano is the moment when he sees the body of his new-born son being dragged away by the ants. In an instant, he understands a key sentence in the manuscripts: 'The first of the line is tied to a tree and the last is being eaten by the ants.' He realizes that the parchments contain a history of his own family, extending over seven generations, from the time of José Arcadio Buendía, who spent the last years of his life in madness, tied to a chestnut tree, down to the death of the final Buendía, his son Aureliano. He realizes, too, that his own destiny will be contained within the manuscripts, and so he withdraws from the world to complete their decipherment. As he reads, the great wind that will destroy Macondo begins to blow around him. He reads of the moment of his own conception, and of his place in the predetermined scheme of things. Everything, he discovers, has been known in advance, and can only end in the way that was foreseen. So that when, in 1595, the English pirate Francis Drake sacked Riohacha, which was then a tiny village of pearl-fishers, hardly bigger than the early Macondo, it was only so that the Buendía story could be set in motion, and so that, in the end, he, Aureliano, would fall in love with his aunt, Amaranta Úrsula, and that, through the intensity of their passion, they would destroy the race of the Buendías.

By now, 'Macondo was already a terrifying whirlwind of dust and rubble being spun about by the wrath of the biblical hurricane', and Aureliano moves on quickly, passionate to know the end. He reaches the point in the manuscripts where he is captured in the very act of deciphering them, a moment of intersection that is pure present, after which, for Aureliano, all is prophecy. He reads on, into the future, but he understands now that he will never leave the room in which he is reading; he has no future beyond the story in which he is a character, and the last sentence of the parchments can only be a sentence of death. On the final page, he discovers, in the words of Emir Rodríguez Monegal, that he is simply 'a ghost who has been dreamed by another man', just a fictional character, 'trapped in a labyrinth of words', and that his fate, completely conterminous with the Macondo that is dying, is to be annihilated so totally that not even a memory will remain.

MICHAEL BELL ON INSOMNIA AND MEMORY

Like some major philosophers, Márquez interprets the mythic Fall from Eden as the cultural fall into dualism; or more precisely the twin dualisms of self versus world and mind versus body. For what has not been sufficiently remarked in the Buendías' shift from Arcadia to history is the fact that the memory loss arises from lack of sleep. They lose the capacity for a recuperative rest from consciousness. In other words, insomnia precedes amnesia and, properly understood, this constitutes a challenge to the well-known philosophical adage of Márquez' own Parisian days, which were the existentialist 1950s rather than the surrealist 1920s, namely the Sartrean formula that 'existence precedes essence'.

Appropriately, the memory sickness, like the pox, is a result of conquest. In the compacted symbolic history of the novel, the disease is rightly caught from the Indian servants since the destruction of someone else's cultural memory usually involves the guilty repression of your own. But the Indians' very form of memory may also have been different from that of their conquerors in being more obviously related to the world of sleep and dream. When the people of Macondo are first told they have the insomnia plague they are more pleased than appalled since they now expect to have more time for their daily activities. But the loss of the apparently useless hours of sleep eventually impairs their capacity to perform even the most necessary functions of everyday life. The daytime self is unwittingly dependent on the night-time self, not just as a period of rest but as an opening to a different order of time and meaning through which the daytime activity itself ultimately needs to be understood.

In other words, the relation of memory and sleep in the double disease suggests that there may be different kinds of memory. There is a rough analogy here with the distinction Proust drew in the personal realm between conscious intentional memory, which is often fallacious, and the unwitting emotional memory that is triggered by chance events and which wells up as a fresh emotional experience in the present. Indeed, the narrator's way of expressing Fernanda's failure to find her wedding ring, has in itself a Proustian ring: '... sin saber que la busqueda de las cosas perdidas está entorpecida por los habitos rutinarios ... ' / '... not knowing that the search for lost things is hindered by habitual routines ... '

In the collective domain, this conscious intentional memory may be akin to the professional activity of historians, while affective memory is more like what Walter Benjamin had in mind when he said: 'To articulate the past historically does not mean to recognize it "the way it really was" (Ranke). It means to seize hold of memory as it flashes up at a moment of danger'. Benjamin was thinking here of history not as an academic discipline but as an immediate living resource and one which is not, in its deepest sources, under conscious control. In this respect the distinction fleshes out Nietzsche's insistence that, for healthy and effective action, it is as important to forget as to remember, and forgetting, even more than memory, must be an effect of time rather than will. To put the point in more homely terms, it is commonly recognised that difficult experiences have, as we say, to be 'slept on' for their longer-term impact to be absorbed and thus to be converted into meaning. This cannot be purely a function of the conscious will.

Borges' story of 'Funes the Memorious', which he himself described as a 'gigantic metaphor for insomnia', is an illuminating inverse of the insomnia and memory sickness. Funes is endowed with a total responsiveness to experience and a complete recall of his past. But this causes insomnia and actually incapacitates him for action and even for thinking. The story is, among other things, an ironic reflection on the arbitrariness of realism and it is appropriate that the narrator's own 'inadequate' memory creates an essentially dream figure in Furies for it is indeed only as an 'unrealistic' dream of Borges himself that Funes can exist for us. The story is, therefore, not only a satire on realism but also the implicit vindication of a different mode of fiction. Something comparable can be seen in *Hundred Years*.

It is significant that during the memory sickness, before the people recover their capacity to function, at least apparently, in the world of daily consciousness, the underlying obsessions of the major characters are overtly dominant. José Arcadio thinks remorsefully of Prudencio Aguilar; Aureliano makes a precious object in his workshop, and Rebeca dreams of her parents. All the characters find themselves, at this time, 'todo el dia soñando despiertos' (p. 120) / 'in a waking dream all day' (p. 44). They believe they have been rescued from this state when Melquíades' potion restores their daytime memory. But in truth they have now lost their capacity properly to inhabit both worlds so that the dream world of their suppressed obsessions henceforth imposes itself on their daytime lives. And Melquíades, who like the great epic heroes has himself visited the world of the dead, now retires to chronicle the working out of the Buendías' unconscious destiny in a language they cannot understand.

In the subsequent story of the Buendías it becomes evident that they have lost their proper access to this other realm of sleep; a realm which is commonly expressed, within the terms of daytime consciousness, through magical and dream images. But the fundamental narrative trick of the book, as fundamental as Alonso Quijano's imagining himself as the fictional character, Don Quixote, is that Márquez goes on to tell their story at the level of the Buendías' repressed selves. The inseparability of the two realms is embodied in the narrative mode as the magical dimension of the narrative enacts the structures of which they are not aware. As will be seen in more detail, the narrative adopts a humorous convention of treating the characters' emotions as physical elements and events in the world, so that they, and we, actually see the magical events and elements, but their awareness is more that of sleep-walkers. Their actions in the daytime world are governed by deep structures within which their conscious world, and our narrative world, remain enclosed.

Several times a character is actually described as being 'like a sleepwalker'. This has usually a Quixotic and partly comic implication although it is pathetic in the eventual case of Meme, who wishes to break out of the emotional enclosure of the Buendías and is shocked into a state of sleepwalking trauma, the extreme form of fixated dream, by Fernanda. The implication is that the dream self needs expression and, if its unconscious working is in sleep, its more conscious arena is the imagination. The relation of dream and fiction is unwittingly recognised by the townsfolk as they seek to recover the world of dream by telling themselves the circular story of the capon. Unfortunately, they see this in a simply utilitarian light as a means of exhaustion and miss the deeper instinct which suggests that a story may indeed be the royal road to the realm of the unconscious. Fiction deals importantly with reality but through the dream as well as the daytime self. For Márquez, no less than Borges, a fiction which merely imitates the daily world is itself an empty, and potentially damaging, illusion.

EDWIN WILLIAMSON ON MAGICAL REALISM

Magical realism creates its aesthetic impact by fusing terms that are in principle opposed to each other. The effect upon the reader of such a fusion of fact and fantasy or innocence and knowledge is, however, not one of absolute identification with the characters but rather a mixed reaction of sympathy and comic detachment. Let us take as an example José Arcadio Buendía's encounter with ice. In the first instance, the narrator describes the ice in a de-familiarizing way which allows the reader to share in the character's wonderment at the mysterious phenomenon:

> When the giant opened it, the chest let out a chilly breath of air. Inside it there was just an enormous transparent block with countless internal needles which broke up the light of the setting sun into stars of many colours. (p. 22)

And yet, when it comes to *explaining* the mystery, the difference between José Arcadio Buendía's innocent awe and the reader's knowledge is sharply drawn within the text itself, producing an effect of comic irony:

> Taken aback, yet knowing that his sons expected an immediate explanation, José Arcadio Buendía dared to murmur, 'It's the biggest diamond in the world.'
>   'No,' the gypsy corrected him, 'it's ice'. (p. 23)

José Arcadio Buendía's awe at the discovery of ice remains unimpaired—he pronounces it 'the greatest invention of our time'—but the reader can no longer share in that response since it is evident that García Márquez intends the gypsy's correction as a signal that the character is touchingly misinterpreting phenomena which the reader is presumed to take for granted in his own experience of the world. The sense of the marvelous afforded us by magical realism is therefore transient, for soon enough García Márquez tips the wink at his reader, as it were, creating a complicity behind the backs of the characters who remain circumscribed by an elemental innocence which charms but is not, of course, meant to convince. Such humorous complicity exists in the more fantastical instances of magical realism, as in, say, Remedios the Beautiful's assumption into heaven in a flurry of white sheets (p. 205). Even though the inhabitants of Macondo might accept this as a true event, as far as the reader is concerned, the fact of its being narrated in the text does not strengthen its claim to literal, historical truth. Rather the opposite, it de-mystifies the phenomenon because of the underlying assumption (as in the ice scene above) that the reader's world-view is at odds with that of the characters.

In spite of its ostensible fusion of fantasy and fact, magical realism is conceived as a wilfully specious discourse that inevitably betrays its hallucinatory character in the very act of its being read by the kind of reader García Márquez is addressing. Were the reader to participate wholly in the perspective of José Arcadio Buendía, there would be no humour in *One Hundred Years of Solitude*; its discourse would be all too solemnly denotative. But García Márquez sets up an ironic interplay between the *identity* of opposites promoted by the magical-real discourse and the inescapable sense of *difference* retained by the reader. The novel is, then, predicated upon a dialectic that opposes the experiences of the world *inside* the fiction to that which lies *outside* it.

MICHAEL WOOD ON LOVE AND SOLITUDE

The cards appear to be stacked against the Buendías in love— or at least against any love which might lead them out of their solitude. Disease and bad luck will ruin romance, even if fear and pride don't, and the sudden death of little Remedios, in particular, would seem savagely gratuitous, like the death of

Cordelia in *King Lear*, if it didn't seem so firmly designed to keep Colonel Aureliano Buendía away from happiness—just in case his solitary character shouldn't entirely do the trick. Meme Buendía, as we have seen, was sociable and in love, had none of the family's supposed vocation for solitude, until an absurd accident masquerading as fate crippled her lover and sent her to a convent. This is a proof either that fate gets you in the end, or that when you are got you call it fate.

The implication then is not of a generalized, Proustian impossibility of love but of something stranger, more restrictive. Aureliano Segundo doesn't get on with his wife Fernanda but finds both passion and calm with Petra Cotes, and the novel is full of warm-hearted, sexually welcoming women—Petra, Pilar Ternera, Santa Sofía de la Piedad, the friendly inhabitants of both real and imaginary brothels—who plainly serve to demystify the dark bolero. They show that love *can* be easy and doom-free, and they are a crucial axis, the relaxed norm against which nightmares are measured. What is significant is that none of them is a Buendía. They are the antithesis of the strict and industrious Úrsula; of the frightened Amaranta; of the unaroused Remedios the Beauty; of the frigid Fernanda, who becomes a Buendía by marriage and also by acceding to what might be called their legacy of solitude.

The family doom thus seems entirely set. There are avoidable destinies in the novel, but this is not one of them. The effect finally is that of a magical rule, something like the prohibition of love in Thomas Mann's *Dr Faustus*. The rule is that races condemned to one hundred years of solitude not only don't have a second opportunity on earth [360: 383], they don't have a chance to love even in their first and only term. They can't love, except in isolated cases which highlight the general force of the rule. This sometimes reflects a fact of character and sometimes a sort of conspiracy of events. In other words the Buendías often can't bring themselves to love, but are also on occasion literally prevented from loving. Simply to say they are incapable of love is to deny the conspiracy against them, to miss the weird collusion between chance and their weakness—chance in novels, we remember, being nothing other than the careful simulation of the unplanned. There are all kinds of obstacles to love for the Buendías, and their variety illustrates the complexity of the point.

The great interest of the stormy romance between Aureliano Babilonia and Amaranta Úrsula, the last couple in the book, is that it threatens to convert solitude into happiness, thereby confounding the whole dark conceptual framework of the fiction. They seem to have found the love that was lacking in the story of Remedios the Beauty, and indeed almost everywhere else, and of course if they have found this love, then the very notion of a magical rule or a family doom evaporates, turns retrospectively into a long but not unending chapter of reclusions and mischances.

We have heard of the 'paradise of shared solitude' [295: 313] which is Aureliano Segundo's and Petra's love, but the key words pile up with feverish intensity, and with new colours, in the last chapter of the novel. Macondo becomes lonely again, 'forgotten even by the birds', and Aureliano and Amaranta Úrsula are 'secluded by solitude and love and by the solitude of love' [349: 371]. They are 'the only happy beings, and the most happy on the face of the earth' [349: 372], a tautology which manages to sound delirious about their happiness. There is a slightly clumsy moralizing in the prose, a clawing back of these characters on to a path of recognizable virtue, when their love is said to settle down—they exchange salacity for solidarity [352: 375], crazy fornication for an affection based on loyalty [355: 378]—but the exhilaration of this last wild adventure remains. Aureliano and Amaranta Úrsula make love in the pool and the patio, break up the furniture and are said to do more damage than the encroaching red ants. They are close to becoming 'a single being', that ultimate creature of incest, and they are 'more and more integrated into the solitude of the house' [354: 376]. Their world is a 'paradise of poverty' [355: 378], a 'paradise of disasters' [350: 373]. There are ambiguities here, of course, and a hint that happy love has its price. The sad words retain their sadness, solitude *is* solitude even if it's bliss, and the world may crumble around you. But by the same token paradise is paradise even if it's a ruin, and the lovers cheerfully pay the price of isolation. Their child is said to be the only infant 'in a century' to be conceived in love [356: 379]—a commentary on and a challenge to the title of the novel. And then the horror strikes, a price of an entirely different kind is exacted. The child has a pig's tail, and Amaranta Úrsula dies soon after bearing him. The child itself, abandoned by Aureliano in his misery, is eaten by the ants.

(...)

The last lovers appear to break the magical rule of *One Hundred Years of Solitude*, and are spectacularly, terminally punished—are punished, I suggest, not for their incest but for being happy in love. I'm tempted to speak of reckless authorial cruelty here, but the narrative gesture is not quite that. Certainly the rule is saved only by the writer's eager insistence on it, but this represents what I take to be a scruple and a conflict. García Márquez can't make his last or any central characters happy, they are Buendías, emblems of a whole charming but imprisoned culture. Yet he really does seem to believe in the unearned, transgressive happiness that Aureliano Babilonia and Amaranta Úrsula achieve, and the haste and harshness with which he recruits and aggravates the old prophecy is a mark of the trouble they are causing. Their crime, I think, is their successful escape from history—the very history everyone else is disastrously forgetting. They almost redeem solitude, and one can see why a novelist, however drawn to them, would hesitate to let them wreck his plot and title and all his moral and political implications. They really need a new novel, they are more than Melquíades or Gabriel bargained for. Perhaps García Márquez was thinking of this effect when he said that his earlier books finished on the last page, belonged to 'a kind of premeditated literature that offers too static and exclusive a vision of reality'.

REGINA JAMES ON BIBLICAL AND HELLENIC DEVICES

The story of Macondo and the Buendías is in part the story of a marginal world recapitulating the experiences of the center, and one of the ways the text acts out that repetition is by recapitulating the literature of the center. Just as José Arcadio Buendía catches up to modernity in his own idiosyncratic way, so this text establishes its modernity by catching up to modern writing in the web formed by Western writing.

To reach its end, *One Hundred Years of Solitude* adopts the narrative frame of the Bible and the plot devices of *Oedipus Tyrannos*, and parodies both. These two founding narratives of Western culture provide a double foundation for the novel, and the echoes of both are pervasive and unmistakable. A family doomed to incest and a fatal baby who will bring the line to an end have only one possible origin—literature. Melquíades, our Delphic oracle, dooms the Buendías to their fate—*fatum*, what is spoken—because he says it and improves on Delphi by writing it down (as biblical prophets did). (The curse is more literary than mythic. Like biblical prophecy, the text is tainted by legitimate suspicions that a later editor has improved the accuracy of the original prophet's words. For the modern reader the Oedipus complex is a myth; fatality is a myth, invoked to dispel chance, but a curse on the house of Laios is not. Confusing the idea of fatality with the literal curse of the Oedipus myth leads to all those readings that make it sound as though García Márquez believes in ancestral curses. What survives as archetypal from that myth is fatality and repressed desire, not a curse of the gods.)

With the (parodic) curse of incest trailing the family, the novel invokes the Hellenic origins of Western culture, as does the name Arcadio, from Arcady, that peaceful, pastoral, isolated world in the mountains of central Greece. Nor is Greek science neglected in favor of Greek literature: it is the learning of Thales, the pre-Socratic philosopher who cornered the olive market, predicted eclipses, and introduced geometry (640?–546 B.C.), that Melquíades first brings to Macondo. "All things are full of Gods," said Thales; "the magnet has a soul because it makes the iron move." Somewhat unexpectedly, the Buendía history as a whole parallels the history of Greece: sixth-century science precedes fifth-century literature, which overlaps with a 20-year civil war, the Peloponnesian War (431–404 B.C.). The end of the democracy and "golden age" is followed by foreign invasions, Alexander's Macedonians, the Romans, the Ottomans, and, ultimately, the cultural collapse that grieved Byron and other nineteenth-century Hellenophiles. In other words, the history of Macondo is paradigmatic: it follows a pattern that has been played out before in human history, and not only by Greece. The Macedonians, Romans, and Ottomans followed it, too, not to speak of the Maya, Bantu, Inca, and Easter Islanders.

More specific to the novel is the Hellenic impact on structure, the parodic literalization of anagnorisis and peripeteia in the conclusion. Aureliano Babilonia "discovers" who his parents are, what his relation to his beloved was, and what the cosmic meaning of their union was. He also discovers that he is a character in a writing who cannot get out, and in that discovery he finds an entirely unexpected "reversal" of fortune. Looking into a speaking mirror, he discovers that the mirror is real and he is not.

With a youthful patriarch and founding couple in a world so new that things lack names, the novel shifts to another fundamental text, the Bible. In so doing, it at once doubles its structural principles. If the Hellenic principle is dynamic, the Hebrew structure is more static—it tells us where we are and when it is over. Biblical allusion pervades the text, and it is especially marked whenever a disaster looms on the horizon.

In an intricate mélange of stories from the Pentateuch, the first page sets us in a pre-Adamic world where things still lack names. In the prehistory of Macondo, Úrsula and José Arcadio Buendía flee from an original crime, a murder (expulsion from the garden), to a land "that no one had promised them," through a mountainous wilderness with a band of followers (the exodus). There, like Cain, they found a city that will later be visited by plagues (insomnia, proliferation of animals, bananas), floods, and an apocalyptic whirlwind that wipes it off the face of the earth. In its earliest moments, before the beginning of this story, the town was happy. José Arcadio Buendía was a youthful patriarch, no one had died, and they had forgotten original sin. When the novel begins, however, the old serpent has bitten José Arcadio Buendía,

106

who lusts for knowledge. Eventually, his wife finds what he has looked for in vain: not only gold but also the road to civilization. Generations later, the story comes to an end in a book that reveals not the future but the past (like Daniel) and seals it up in a book, like Revelation or Daniel.

By invoking the Bible, García Márquez seems to be invoking the origin of all origins, an absolutely primary time; but for anyone familiar with the textual history of the Bible, to invoke the Bible as *the* beginning is to evoke an endless regress of texts, redactions, and fictive authors. Critics have hastened to point out that there is no primary time in *One Hundred Years of Solitude*. The gypsies show that knowledge, science, society, all exist elsewhere, and that Macondo's experience is not primary but a repetition. The skeleton and the galleon not only confirm that there is a world elsewhere, but they also show that people like the *macondanos* once passed where Macondo now is.

At the metatextual level, the very recognition that Macondo is new depends upon a quotation, a reference to a prior text. That sense of newness, of recent creation, of absolute origins, is an illusion. As far as I know, however, no critic has pointed out that in the Bible, too, the beginning is not the beginning. The first words are not the oldest words in the text or the first words of the world, and this primary, original text is in fact a highly complex editing of many vanished texts. Even more to the point. the first five books of the text are traditionally attributed to an author whose life story, including his death, is told inside those five books.

BRIAN CONNIFF ON MAGIC, SCIENCE, AND TRAGEDY IN THE NOVEL

The tragedy of José Arcadio Buendía is that his infatuation with science allows the government to exploit a passion that was, initially, a "spirit of social initiative." His first creations were the traps and cages he used to fill all the houses in the village with birds. He made sure that the houses were placed "in such a way that from all of them one could reach the river and draw water with the same effort" (18); he saw that no house received more sun than another. He was, from the start, a type of "model citizen," useful to his people. It is the appearance of "advanced" science in Macondo that makes him, virtually overnight, useful to authority: "That spirit of social initiative disappeared in a short time, pulled away by the fever of magnets, the astronomical calculations, the dreams of transmutation, and the urge to discover the wonders of the world" (18). That is how his faith in progress, and the faith of his people, is betrayed.

But more important than José Arcadio's tragic disappointment, more important than his invested dubloons—which Melquíades returns in any case—even more important than his final senility, is the fact that he resolves his debate with the gypsy. Throughout the rest of the novel, scientific discoveries will continue to serve two purposes: science will mystify the citizens of Macondo and will lead to their exploitation. The novel's arresting first sentence suggests that these two purposes have always been inseparable: "Many years later, as he faced the firing squad, Colonel Aureliano Buendía was to remember that distant afternoon when his father took him to discover ice" (11). But, perhaps, if his father had avoided such discoveries, Aureliano Buendía might never have wound up before a firing squad of his own government.

The equally arresting ending of the novel is a full-scale denial of José Arcadio's ill-begotten dream. The novel's "apocalyptic closure" is a denial of progress, as conceived by either the scientist or the politician, and a momentary glimpse of the world that might have been, if the great patriarch had not been so carried away with his idea of the future—if he had tried, instead, to understand history. Only Amaranta Úrsula and Aureliano, the last adults in the line of the Buendías, see "the uncertainty of the future" with enough demystified clarity to forsake progress,"to turn their hearts toward the past"; only they are not exploited (375). Their child, Aureliano, is "the only one in a century who had been engendered with love"—but by then it is too late (378). They cannot enjoy their primal, "dominant obsessions" for long; they cannot remain "floating in an empty universe where the only everyday and eternal reality was love" (374). They are confronted, instead, with an end that is as ridiculous as their family's beginning: "The first of the line is tied to a tree and the last is being eaten by the ants" (381). The world has not progressed one bit. In fact, the key to understanding the present, and all of history, is not in the science so valued by José Arcadio but in Melquíades's ancient manuscripts, written in Sanskrit. Macondo is finally devoured by the "prehistoric hunger" of the ants, then obliterated by "the wrath of the biblical hurricane" (383).

Because he is the man of technology, the man of science-as-progress, who brings together, more than anyone else, mystification and exploitation, José Arcadio is never able to foresee this end, just as he is never able to turn his obsessive nature toward love, just as he is never able to admit the kind of association that occurs to Colonel Aureliano Buendía when he faces the firing squad. He never understands, as Úrsula does, that time is circular. He never really pays any attention to the suit of armor from the past, so he never learns that the rusted coat of armor anticipates the soldiers and machine guns that will support the banana company, that the imperialism of the past prefigures the imperialism of the future. In this sense, Úrsula is capable of learning; José Arcadio is not. Úrsula learns, at least, that her schemes for prosperity have set her up to be betrayed. Ultimately, José Arcadio cannot understand any of these things because his view of the world shares too much with the oppressors who will take over his village in the delirium of banana fever; in other words, whether he realizes it or not, his horizon is determined by the interests he serves. As John Incledon has written, José Arcadio's fascination with scientific inventions—as sources of wealth, power, control—"reveals a frantic desire to grasp and manage his world" (53).

IRIS M. ZAVALA ON THE GEOGRAPHY AND ISOLATION OF MACONDO

The chapters do not follow a linear structure but rather present several plots that, with leaps forward and backward in time, interweave the past history of each character. The sequence is neither chronological nor logical; the reader fulfills the function of an historian, with facts and lives being set in order. The first five chapters describe the idyllic phase of Macondo, its genesis. The small settlement, "una aldea de veinte casas de barro y cañabrava construidas a la orilla de un rio con aguas diáfanas" (a village of twenty adobe houses, built on the bank of a river of clear water, grows and evolves gradually before our eyes. Macondo is a center colonized by pilgrims who herald from elsewhere. Some, like José Arcadio Buendía and Úrsula, are fleeing the past; others join in for the sake of adventure and to test their luck. They will all be the future aristocracy.

Despite the settlers' isolation, the references to the world outside are fairly constant. Difficult access notwithstanding, one day Melquíades's tribe arrives at the village, led by bird calls. Melquíades dazzles José Arcadio Buendía; he speaks of Macedonia, of distant civilizations. He has died many times and, as frequently, has lived again, always being reborn and always elderly, as indicated by the name of his tribe: the Naciancenes, undoubtedly a reminiscence of St. Gregory Nazianzus, often cited by the chroniclers. Melquíades signifies progress; with him there arrives word of inventions and discoveries, already old news across the swamp from Macondo, but unsuspected in the town, where everything is anachronistic and arrives ill timed. The gypsy brings the magnifying glass, the astrolabe, and alchemy.

José Arcadio Buendía is seduced by a hunger for knowledge and the fascination of science. "En el mundo están ocurriendo cosas increibles. Ahí mismo, al otro lado del rio, hay toda cease de aparatos mágicos, mientras nosotros seguimos viviendo como burros" (15) [Incredible things are happening in the world. Right there across the river there are all kinds of magical instruments while we keep on living like donkeys (17)]. José Arcadio, the patriarch, the founder, who decides and organizes and creates everything in his own image and likeness and under whose leadership the streets had been traced and the settlement transformed into a great, orderly, hard-working village, will stray ever further from his prime spirit of social initiative. Old Buendía is seized by a rage for magnets, for astronomical computations, for dreams of transmuting metals, an insatiable thirst to know all of the world's marvels. The seeker of progress cuts himself off from reality, increasingly convinced that knowledge equals superiority. He wishes to learn from Nature the way to harness it in order to gain total domination of the universe. Power and knowledge for him are synonymous; knowing equals controlling. In his hands the magnifying glass becomes a battlefield weapon, and he composes a manual that he sends to the authorities for the purposes of putting it in the hands of the military and training them in "las complicadas artes de la guerra solar" (11) [the complicated art of solar war (13)].

Melquíades—the Enlightenment, science, knowledge for knowledge's sake—attempts to dissuade him, without success. The alchemy lab becomes in José Arcadio Buendía's hands a money-minting machine; Úrsula's colonial coins have to be multiplied as many times as one can subdivide quicksilver (CAS, 14; OYS, 12).

The discovery of ice makes him think of transforming the geography and the climate—building houses made of ice, fantastical igloos in a torrid zone that would cease to be a sweltering spot and turn into a wintry city. The subject of ice is one of the central ideas in the book; in the dream of José Arcadio Buendía, Macondo is a city with frozen mirrors on its house walls. In Macondo, as in Spanish America, everything is but a reflection of the real, and its dwellers copy, seek progress elsewhere, imitate, and do not create. Everything has always been imported—first by the tribe of Melquíades, later by the Banana Company, which transforms the town and makes it "naufragar en una prosperidad de milagro" (168), or, as the English version puts it, has Macondo "swamped in a miraculous prosperity" (185).

Avid for progress and science, José Arcadio Buendía requests "el concurso de todos para abrir una trocha que pusiera a Macondo con los grandes inventos" (16) [the assembled group to open a way that would put Macondo in contact with the great inventions (19)]. Symbolically, this would be the northward route; the East leads to the past, to the former town of Riohacha; to the South there was the great swamp; and the North was "la única posibilidad de contacto con la civilizatión" (17) (the only possibility of contact with civilization (19)]. The reckless adventure of José Arcadio Buendía will lead them to a place where "el mundo se volvió triste para siempre" (17) [the world became eternally sad (20)]. There they find a paradise of humidity and silence, prior to original sin, where their boots sink and their machetes destroy bloody irises and golden salamanders. With their lungs overwhelmed by the suffocating odor of blood and their lives totally dependent on the compass, one morning they find a Spanish galleon, symbol of the colony. Macondo, Spanish America, is a solitary colony and, worst of all, is an island. José Arcadio Buendía's exclamation—"¡Carajo! Macondo está rodeado de aqua por todas partes" (18) [God damn it! Macondo is surrounded by water on all sides (21)]— takes us back to the old Renaissance concept of island versus continent. For the first navigators, continents were only those lands within the *orbis terrarum*—Europe and the Mediterranean. The word "continent" had at the time a denotation that was purely cultural and historical, not geographical. The insular Macondo hence doesn't belong to the West; it is not part of the European world but rather is an isolated place, incapable of achieving the progress that comes from the North, where there are tramways, postal services, and machines. Doubtless, a pointless land that has been ill born! Since the Conquest it has aroused only unbridled greed. How regretfully did the good Father Bartolomé las Casas exclaim that in this New World all was plagues and death:

So much damage! So many calamities! So many kingdoms depopulated! So many stories of souls! ... So many and such unforgivable sins have been committed! So much blindness, and such disregard of conscience!

It is Úrsula who will find the way to the outside world. After disappearing for five months, she returns with "hombres y mujeres como ellos, de cabellos lacios y piel parda, que hablaban su misma lengua y se lamentaban de los mismos dolores" [men and women like them, with straight hair and dark skin, who spoke the same language and complained of the same pains]. Incredibly, "[v]enían del otro lado de la ciénaga, a solo dos días de viaje, donde había pueblos que recibian el correo todos los meses y conocian todas las máquinas del bienestar" (38) [they came from the other side of the swamp, only two days away, where there were towns that received mail every month in the year and where they were familiar with the implements of good living (43)].

On Úrsula's return the inhabitants are stricken with the insomnia plague, which produces forgetfulness and makes everyone see the dreams of others. The allegory is clear: Macondo, America, is a mirage, a dream. Everything repeats itself in a constant circle. The José Arcados and the Aurelianos are always the same ones, united, like the twins of Arcadio and Santa Sofía de la Piedad, their identities blurred even in death. Time always spins on itself. The history of the family is a machine with unavoidable repetitions, a turning wheel whose axle gradually wears out. Úrsula reiterates it several times: "Es como si el tiempo diera vueltas en redondo y hubiéramos vuelto al principio" (169, 192, 285) [It's as if time had turned around and we were back at the beginning" (185, 209, 310)]. America is an anachronistic land, a journey inside-out of time. Once again García Márquez coincides with Martinez Estrada, who explains the discovery voyage by saying, "Each day of navigation the caravels retraced one hundred years. The voyage was made across the ages, receding from the epoch of the compass and of the printing press to that of chiseled stone." The continent is an old land where nothing new takes place, and where what is reproduced are merely the personal variants of many histories now long forgotten.

Works by Gabriel García Márquez

(listed in order of English-language publication)

No One Writes to the Colonel and Other Stories, 1968.

One Hundred Years of Solitude, 1970.

Leaf Storm and Other Stories, 1972.

The Autumn of the Patriarch, 1976.

Innocent Eréndira and Other Stories, 1978.

In Evil Hour, 1979.

Chronicle of a Death Foretold, 1982.

The Story of a Shipwrecked Sailor, 1986.

Clandestine in Chile: The Adventures of Miguel Littin, 1987.

Love in the Time of Cholera, 1988.

The General in His Labyrinth, 1990.

Strange Pilgrims, 1993.

Of Love and Other Demons, 1995.

News of a Kidnapping, 1997.

Living to Tell the Tale, 2003.

Memories of My Melancholy Whores, 2005.

Annotated Bibliography

Anderson, Jon Lee, "The Power of Gabriel García Márquez," *The New Yorker*, September 27, 1999.

Anderson's article is a profile that focuses on Márquez's international reputation, and whether it has any practical applications for the political world today.

Bell, Michael, *Gabriel García Márquez: Solitude and Solidarity*, London: Macmillian Press, 1993.

An informative survey of Márquez's work, with a focus on *One Hundred Years of Solitude*, which, as Bell and other critics stress, is positive in Márquez's universe. The chapter devoted to *One Hundred Years* is particularly interesting for its discussion on Melquíades, and also its discussion of the importance of the insomnia plague.

Bell-Villada, Gene H., *García Márquez: The Man and His Work*, Chapel Hill, North Carolina: University of North Carolina Press, 1990.

The chapter entitled "The Readings" provides a good overview of early influences on Márquez, like Kafka, the Bible, Greek drama, and Faulkner. Also, "History of Macondo" provides a clear synopsis of *One Hundred Years* while discussing it in terms of myth, historical context, and literary precedents.

Bell-Villada, Gene H. (ed.), *Gabriel García Márquez's* One Hundred Years of Solitude: *A Casebook*. New York. Oxford University Press, 2002.

An interesting, well-thought-out collection, which covers many aspects, including various feminist and political-historical readings. Bell-Villada, the editor, also publishes English translations of important Latin American essays.

Bell-Villada, Gene H., "Banana Strike and Military Massacre: *One Hundred Years of Solitude* and What Happened in 1928,"

In *From Dante to García Márquez: Studies in Romance Literature and Linguistics*, Gene Bell-Villada, Antonio Gimenez, and George Pistorius, ed. Williamstown, Massachussetts: Williams College, 1987, pp. 391–402.

Bell-Villada discusses the 1928 banana massacre, which occurred next door to Márquez's village during the author's infancy, and that makes a significant appearance at the end of *One Hundred Years*.

Conniff, Brian, "The Dark Side of Magical Realism: Science, Oppression, and Apocalpyse in *One Hundred Years of Solitude*," *Modern Fiction Studies 36* (1990) 167–179.

Conniff makes the point that with recent science, the twisted absurd things suggested by magical realism—including the end of the world—become increasingly possible, a fact that Márquez is keenly aware of.

Fuentes, Carlos, "García Márquez: On Second Reading," in *La nueva novela Hispanoamericana*, Mexico: Joaquin Mortia, 1970, pp. 58–67.

The first reading of *One Hundred Years*, Fuentes argues, is as a chronological history. The second reading is as simultaneous myth, and therefore the experience of *One Hundred Years* lies in the tension between the two.

Gallagher, D.P., "Gabriel García Márquez," in D.P. Gallagher, *Modern Latin American Literature*, Oxford: Oxford University Press, 1973, pp. 144–163.

Focusing on *One Hundred Years* on the heels of its publication, Gallagher's chapter is a contemporary critique that already treats the book with mythological proportions. He even goes so far as to argue that Márquez may have actually surpassed Nabokov in the way it has swallowed literary and historical tradition.

García Márquez, Gabriel, *Living to Tell the Tale*, Edith Grossman, trans., New York: Alfred A. Knopf, 2003.

Márquez's fascinating first volume of his autobiography provides plenty of details about his life in Aracataca, which would later be the material for *One Hundred Years*.

Guibert, Rita, "Gabriel García Márquez," in *Seven Voices: Seven Latin American Writers Talk to Rita Guibert*, trans. Frances Partridge, New York: Alfred A. Knopf, 1973.

Guibert is a well-known literary journalist whose interview portrays Márquez as an anti-intellectual.

Higgins, James, "Gabriel García Márquez: *Cien años de soledad*," in *Landmarks in Modern Latin American Fiction*, Philip Swanson, ed., New York: Routlege, 1990, pp. 141–160.

An excellent summary of *One Hundred Years of Solitude*, that relates the novel to Márquez's own life.

James, Regina, *Gabriel García Márquez: Revolutions in Wonderland*, Columbia and London: University of Missouri Press, 1981.

Included is a competent biography of the author and his relationship to Colombia—and also an introduction to El Boom, the Latin American literary movement. James also provides a map of Márquez's creative maturity. In terms of *One Hundred Years of Solitude*, she has the clearest discussion of structure.

James, Regina, One Hundred Years of Solitude: *Modes of Reading*, Boston: Twayne Publishers, 1991.

Here James deals with themes of incest and politics, but is most thorough on the different texts that Márquez draws on in his novel.

McGuirk, Bernard and Richard A. Cardwell, ed., *Gabriel García Márquez: New Readings*, New York: Cambridge University Press, 1987.

Perhaps the most consistently illuminating collection of essays to be published on Márquez, published to coincide with Márquez's winning of the Nobel Prize. Included is a good essay by Gonzalez on the theme of genealogy in *One Hundred Years*, as well as an essay by Clive Griffin (later collected in Bell-Vidalia, *One Hundred Years: A Casebook*) on the theme of humor. Another standout is Edwin Williamson's essay on magical realism and incest.

McMurray, George R., *Gabriel García Márquez* (Modern Literature Monographs), New York: Frederick Ungar Publishing Co., 1977.

McMurray's Márquez book contains a thorough chronology of the author's life. Easy-to-read chapters document Márquez's psychological and artistic development, which culminated in *One Hundred Years*. "Myth and Reality, a Perfect Synthesis" argues precisely what its title implies—that in his seminal novel, Márquez was finally able to refine fantasy by combining it with journalistic fact.

McNerney, Kathleen, *Understanding Gabriel García Márquez*, Columbia, South Carolina: University of South Carolina Press, 1989.

McNerney's survey includes a good overview of Márquez's relationship with Colombia, and also a thorough discussion on the incorporation of past and contemporary works into the text of *One Hundred Years*.

Mendoza, Plinio Apuleyo, *The Fragrance of the Guava*, *Plinio Apuleyo Mendoza in Conversation with Gabriel García Márquez*, trans. Thomas Nairn, London: Verso, 1963.

In this volume, two writers and friends discuss the creative process.

Minta, Stephen, *Gabriel García Márquez: Writer of Colombia*, London: Jonathan Cape, 1987.

Minta's is probably the most thorough analysis of Márquez's work in a socio-political context. Two chapters provide two different readings for *One Hundred Years*—literary, and historical.

Ortega, Julio and Claudia Elliot (ed.), *Gabriel García Márquez and the Powers of Fiction*, Austin: University of Texas Press, 1988.

Includes several essays that touch upon *One Hundred Years*, as well as the famous Nobel Prize acceptance address that Márquez delivered in 1988, where he talks about world peace and poetry. Aníbel González's discussion on the influence of journalism on Márquez is particularly useful.

Paternostro, Silva, "Three Days with Gabo," in *Latin American Writers at Work*, George Plimpton, ed., New York: Modern Library, 2003, pp. 155–181.

A journalist's account of attending the workshop that Márquez began in 1995 for writers.

Stone, Peter H., "Gabriel García Márquez," in *Latin American Writers at Work*, George Plimpton, ed., New York: Modern Library, 2003, pp. 127–154.

Stone's piece is a seminal interview about the writing of *One Hundred Years of Solitude*. Márquez discusses the influence of journalism, its beginnings with *La Casa*, and his personal take on the Latin American response to its publication and on his subsequent fame.

Williams, Raymond L., *Gabriel García Márquez*, Boston: Twayne Publishers, 1984.

The chapter about *One Hundred Years* provides a good summary, along with a competent discussion of its social and political ramifications. William's most insightful point is how the everyday is presented as extraordinary and vice versa.

Wood, Michael, *Gabriel García Márquez:* One Hundred Years of Solitude (Landmarks of World Literature), New York: Cambridge University Press, 1990.

Wood's book is a brief and quite lyrically written basic analysis of *One Hundred Years*. Though Wood's ambitions are modest, the issues upon which he touches—the character of Colonel

Aureliano Buendía, and the nature of love, solitude, and destiny—are superb. He writes especially well upon the relationship among romance, dancing, happiness, and death— as well as about Márquez's relationship to his own characters.

Zamora, Lois Parkinson, "Apocalypse and Human Time in the Fiction of Gabriel García Márquez," in *Writing the Apocalypse: Historical Vision in Contemporary U.S. and Latin American Fiction*, New York: Cambridge University Press, 1989.

Zamora discusses the ending of *One Hundred Years* in terms of apocalypse, in relation to both the Bible and Colombian history.

Zavala, Iris M., "*One Hundred Years of Solitude* as a Chronicle of the Indies," trans. Gene H. Bell-Villada. *Homenaje a Gabriel García Márquez*, Helmy E. Giocaman, ed., New York: Las Americas, 1972, pp. 200–212.

Iris Zavala offers a historical perspective of *One Hundred Years*, arguing that in the Hispano-Caribbean area, forgetting an event is the equivalent of an event's never having happened in the first place.

Contributors

Harold Bloom is Sterling Professor of the Humanities at Yale University. He is the author of 30 books, including *Shelley's Mythmaking* (1959), *The Visionary Company* (1961), *Blake's Apocalypse* (1963), *Yeats* (1970), *A Map of Misreading* (1975), *Kabbalah and Criticism* (1975), *Agon: Toward a Theory of Revisionism* (1982), *The American Religion* (1992), *The Western Canon* (1994), and *Omens of Millennium: The Gnosis of Angels, Dreams, and Resurrection* (1996). *The Anxiety of Influence* (1973) sets forth Professor Bloom's provocative theory of the literary relationships between the great writers and their predecessors. His most recent books include *Shakespeare: The Invention of the Human* (1998), a 1998 National Book Award finalist, *How to Read and Why* (2000), *Genius: A Mosaic of One Hundred Exemplary Creative Minds* (2002), *Hamlet: Poem Unlimited* (2003), *Where Shall Wisdom Be Found?* (2004), and *Jesus and Yahweh: The Names Divine* (2005). In 1999, Professor Bloom received the prestigious American Academy of Arts and Letters Gold Medal for Criticism. He has also received the International Prize of Catalonia, the Alfonso Reyes Prize of Mexico, and the Hans Christian Andersen Bicentennial Prize of Denmark.

Lorraine Elena Roses is Professor of Latin American Studies and of Spanish at Wellesley College. She is the co-author of *Harlem Renaissance and Beyond: Literary Biographies of 100 Black Woman Writers* and the author of *Voices of the Storyteller: Cuba's Lino Novás Calvo*.

Clive Griffin is Lecturer in Latin American Literature and a Fellow of Trinity College, Oxford. His most recent book is *Journeymen-Printers, Heresy, and the Inquisition in Sixteenth-Century Spain*.

Peter H. Stone has been a staff correspondent for *National Journal* in Washington since 1992 where he has covered a wide array of lobbying and campaign finance issues. He is writing a book on Jack Abramoff and the Indian casino lobbying scandal that is scheduled to be published in the fall of 2006 by Farrar, Straus and Giroux.

Gene H. Bell-Villada is Professor and Chair of Romance Languages and Literatures at Williams College. He is the author of *Arts for Art's Sake & Literary Life*, and also of the novel *The Pianist Who Liked Ayn Rand*.

Aníbal González teaches at the University of Texas, Austin. He has authored articles on Rafael Sanchez, the *cronica modernista*, and also the book, *La novela modernista Hispanoamericana*.

Stephen Minta is a professor at the University of York, specializing in French, Spanish, and Greek. He is the author of *Aguirre: The Re-Creation of a Sixteenth-Century Journey Across South America* and *On a Voiceless Shore: Byron in Greece*.

Michael Bell is a professor at the University of Warwick. He is author of, among other things, *Sentimentalism, Ethics, and the Culture of Feeling* and *Literature, Modernity and Myth*.

Edwin Williamson is a lecturer at Birbeck College, University of London. His focus is on sixteenth- and seventeenth-century Spain, and he has published a book on Cervantes.

Michael Wood is Professor of English and Comparative Literature at Princeton. He has written on Stendhal, Kafka, Márquez, and film, and he writes for publications like *The New Republic* and *The New York Review of Books*.

Regina James is a professor at Skidmore University and has written articles on subjects as diverse as John Gay, J.M. Coetzee, and Carlos Fuentes. She is the author of *Edmund*

Burke on Irish Affairs and *Losing Our Heads: Beheadings in Literature and Culture.*

Brian Conniff is Chair of the Department of English and Associate Professor of English at the Univeristy of Dayton. In addition to his writing on Márquez, Conniff's works include essays on Robert Hayden; prison literature; and the book *The Lyric and Modern Poetry: Olson, Creeley, Bunting.*

Iris M. Zavala has taught in universities in Mexico, New York, Holland, Puerto Rico, and Italy. She has won numerous awards, namely for her books *Ideologia y politica en la novela espanola del siglo XIX; El bolero: Historia de un amor;* and *El libro de Apolonia o de las isles.* She has published numerous articles in English, Spanish, Italian, and French.

Acknowledgments

"The Sacred Harlots of *One Hundred Years of Solitude*" by Lorraine Elena Roses. From *Gabriel García Márquez's* One Hundred Years of Solitude: *A Casebook*, edited by Gene H. Bell-Villada. Oxford University Press, 2002, pp. 67–77. Copyright © 2002 by Oxford University Press, Inc. Used by permission of Oxford University Press, Inc.

"The Humour of *One Hundred Years of Solitude*" by Clive Griffin. From *Gabriel García Márquez: New Readings*, edited by Bernard McGuirk and Richard Cardwell. Cambridge University Press, 1987, pp. 82–85. © 1987 Cambridge University Press. Reprinted with the permission of Cambridge University Press.

"Interview with Gabriel García Marquez" by Peter H. Stone. From *Latin American Writers at Work*, Modern Library, 2003, pp. 138–141. First published in *The Art of Fiction* No. 69 issue: 82 Winter 1981 © 1981 by *The Paris Review*, permission of The Wylie Agency.

"Banana Strike and Military Massacre *One Hundred Years of Solitude* and What Happened in 1928" by Gene H. Bell-Villada. From *Gabriel García Márquez's* One Hundred Years of Solitude: *A Casebook*, edited by Gene H. Bell-Villada. Oxford University Press, 2002, pp. 130–132. Copyright © 2002 by Oxford University Press, Inc. Used by permission of Oxford University Press, Inc.

"The Ends of the Text: Journalism in the Fiction of Gabriel García Márquez" by Aníbal González. From *Gabriel García Marquez and the Powers of Fiction*, edited by Julio Ortega, with the assistance of Claudia Elliott. University of Texas Press, 1988, pp. 61–66. Copyright © 1988. By permission of the University of Texas Press.

Index

Characters in literary works are indexed by first name (if any), followed by the name of the work in parentheses

marriage to Amaranta Úrsula, 32, 71–73
return to Brussels, 73–74
Gerineldo Márquez (*One Hundred Years of Solitude*)
  courtship with Amaranta, 27, 51–52, 60, 65, 83
  death, 65
  military, 47, 50–52, 54
Gravity's Rainbow (Pynchon), 9

H

Hellenic devices in *One Hundred Years of Solitude*, 104–7
Heraldo, El (newspaper), 91
Herbert, Mr. (*One Hundred Years of Solitude*)
  banana factory, 20, 59–60, 89
Homer, 7
  The Odyssey, 18
Hopscotch (Cortázar), 18
Humor in *One Hundred Years of Solitude*
  death and religion, 82–85
  and fantasy, 101
  language and dialogue, 83
  sexual and bodily functions, 82–85, 99

I

Incestuous themes in *One Hundred Years of Solitude*
  with Amaranta Úrsula and Aureliano Babilonia, 32, 74–76, 104
  with Aureliano José and Amaranta, 28, 52, 82
  fantasies, 82–83
  and pig-tailed children, 24, 32, 37, 64, 74–76, 85, 104–5
  with Rebeca and José Arcadio, 46, 48
  Úrsula's fight against, 25, 32, 37–38, 46, 48
In Evil Hour
  language in, 92
  plagues in, 87
  travels to Paris in, 14
  writing, 85

Infante, Guillermo Cabrera, 9
Innocent Eréndira and Other Stories, 18, 41

J

José Arcadio (*One Hundred Years of Solitude*)
  children, 25, 27, 38–39, 48
  death, 26, 50–51, 59, 83
  marriage to Rebeca, 26, 46, 48, 50–51, 74, 76, 80, 82
  parents, 25–26, 37–38, 45
  and Pilar Ternera, 38–40, 48, 79, 81
  prostitution, 26, 46
  sexual endowment, 38, 82
  travels, 21, 26, 39, 45, 84
José Arcadio (II) (*One Hundred Years of Solitude*)
  and Amaranta, 31, 70, 82
  appetites and sins of, 32, 71, 74
  death, 32, 71, 74
  invalid, 31, 70
  parents, 31, 54, 61
  seminary, 31, 61, 70–71, 83, 85
José Arcadio Buendía (*One Hundred Years of Solitude*), 85
  children, 25–27, 33, 37–40, 45
  death, 51, 76, 83
  fight with Apolinar Moscote, 19–20, 26, 41
  founder of Macondo, 10, 24, 35–38, 110, 112
  and the ghosts, 24, 37, 43, 48, 51, 98
  insanity, 24, 34, 43–44, 48, 66, 74, 95, 108
  love of science and exploration, 24, 33, 35–36, 39–40, 42, 55, 59, 69–70, 74, 100–1, 105–11
  murderer, 24, 37, 43, 106
  tied to tree, 24, 44–45, 48, 51, 64, 74, 76, 95
José Arcadio Segundo (*One Hundred Years of Solitude*), 82
  and the banana company massacre, 30, 64, 93, 95
  death, 30, 69, 83, 113

133

134